101 ESSENTIAL LIFE SKILLS FOR TEENS

HOW TO BECOME CONFIDENT AND INDEPENDENT

J.R. BEEL

© Copyright 2023 - **All rights reserved.**

The content contained within this book may not be reproduced, duplicated or transmitted without direct written permission from the author or the publisher.

Under no circumstances will any blame or legal responsibility be held against the publisher, or author, for any damages, reparation, or monetary loss due to the information contained within this book, either directly or indirectly.

Legal Notice:

This book is copyright protected. It is only for personal use. You cannot amend, distribute, sell, use, quote or paraphrase any part, or the content within this book, without the consent of the author or publisher.

Disclaimer Notice:

Please note the information contained within this document is for educational and entertainment purposes only. All effort has been executed to present accurate, up to date, reliable, complete information. No warranties of any kind are declared or implied. Readers acknowledge that the author is not engaged in the rendering of legal, financial, medical or professional advice. The content within this book has been derived from various sources. Please consult a licensed professional before attempting any techniques outlined in this book.

By reading this document, the reader agrees that under no circumstances is the author responsible for any losses, direct or indirect, that are incurred as a result of the use of the information contained within this document, including, but not limited to, errors, omissions, or inaccuracies.

CONTENTS

Introduction	7
1. THINKING SKILLS	13
Thinking Outside of the Box	14
The Power of Reason	15
Making the Right Choices	17
If There's a Problem, There's a Solution!	19
Speak Your Mind	20
Chapter 1 Reflection	22
2. COMMUNICATION SKILLS	27
On the Right Path	28
Becoming a Social Butterfly	29
Talk the Talk	31
Listening to Understand	32
No Man Is an Island	34
The Body Talks	35
Respect Matters	37
Chapter 2 Reflection	38
3. EMOTIONAL SKILLS	43
No More Excuses!	44
Mental Health, It's a Thing	45
From Overwhelmed to Empowered	47
Feeling Alone… It's Okay!	49
It's Okay to Not Be Okay	50
Be True, Be You	51
Let it Out!	53
Heart and Mind	54
Feeling Feelings	56
Healing From the Hurt	57
Embracing Your Awesomeness	58

Count Your Blessings	60
Walk in Their Shoes	62
Speak Your Truth	63
One Compassionate Act at a Time	65
Tolerating Rejection	67
Support, Not Pressure	68
Mind Over Matter	70
Practicing Mindfulness	72
Chapter 3 Reflection	73
4. PERSONAL SKILLS	79
The Power of Not Giving Up	80
Focusing on Yourself	81
Healthy Relationships	82
How to Talk on the Phone	83
Setting Healthy Boundaries	84
Protect Yourself	86
Time Management	88
Being Flexible or Patient	89
Allotting Time for Adequate Sleep	91
The Power of Your Choice	92
Setting Goals	94
Move it Move it	95
Nurturing Your Body	97
Taking Effective Action	99
It Takes a Village	100
Accept Without Judgment	101
Being Responsible!	103
Stronger Than You Think	104
Knowing Your Core Values	105
Stay in Course	107
Understanding the Changes in Your Body	108
Personal Grooming and Hygiene	110
Manners Maketh Man	111
Finding Your Passion	112
The Value of Teamwork	114

Leading Others	115
Stay in School!	117
Homework Responsibilities	118
Use Standard Software	119
Finding an Appropriate Job	119
How to Dress for Success	120
Date Safely!	122
Rock Your Vote	123
Using Technology	124
Limiting Screen Time	126
Social Media Awareness	127
Chapter 4 Reflection	129
5. MONEY SKILLS	133
Why Save Your Money?	134
The Value of Money	135
Financial Self-Discipline	136
How Much Are These?	137
Budgeting Basics	138
Earning and Managing an Allowance	139
Smart Spending	140
Understanding Credit Cards	142
What are Credit Scores?	143
Leaving a Tip	144
Avoiding Debt	146
Understanding Student Loans	147
Learning About Taxes	149
Growing Your Money	151
Stashing Your Cash	152
Getting Insured	153
Chapter 5 Reflection	154
6. HOUSEHOLD SKILLS	159
Flex Your Reflexes	160
Basic First Aid	161
How to Be a Fur-Parent	162
Babysitting Do's and Don'ts	163

Learn to Swim	164
Kitchen Basics	166
How to Cook	168
Reading Nutrition Labels	169
Doing the Laundry	170
Packing a Suitcase	171
Organization Skills	172
Yard Work	174
Basic Housekeeping Skills	175
Unclogging a Toilet or Sink	176
Knowing What Snail Mail is!	177
When GPS Fails, Know How to Read a Map	178
Learning to Drive	179
Young Mechanic	181
Chapter 6 Reflection	182
Conclusion	187
References	191

INTRODUCTION

> *Success depends on previous preparation and without such previous preparation there is sure to be failure.*
>
> — CONFUCIUS

Picture this: It's 20 years from now. Not only did you make it through your teenage years, but your 20s and maybe even 30s have almost passed. Your life is everything you ever dreamed of it being. What does that scene look like? Who are you with? What do you have and what are you doing?

In this world, what steps were taken to get there?

The path to the future we want doesn't always look as pretty as what's waiting at the end. As a teenager, the possibility of what your future might look like is endless. While this is one of the most exciting parts of being an adolescent, it's equally as terrifying. Knowing how to take the right steps toward the future you want is the biggest challenge you'll face as a teen. Fortunately for you, this technological age provides us with endless resources to learn from those who have already gone through what you are about to endure.

TODAY'S YOUTH

A 2021 survey found that out of 1,000 parents, 900 believe their teens lack domestic skills. Only a third of teens between 13-19 knew how to make a bed, with even fewer knowing how to clean a toilet and fold clothes (Winter, 2021).

In the age of the internet, why does it matter if we know these things? You can Google any information you need, *right?*

While that can help if you're looking for a good recipe or researching information for a school paper, not everything can be learned on the fly. Preparing for the years ahead will not only help if you ever find yourself in a sticky situation, but it will give you the confidence to know that you'll be able to work through any challenge that gets tossed your way. Some things will only be learned through experience and time, but the more prepared you are for the future, the easier it will be to power through the times when hard lessons are learned.

Throughout your teenage years, your parents will be less present over time. Starting a job and going to college are two things that you will be responsible for, so while our guardians can guide us in some situations, there will be many that we'll have to go through on our own.

You've learned plenty about navigating life through your teachers, parents, and peers. Though you have a collection of life experiences already, this guide is here to fill in the gaps.

101 Essential Skills

This is not your usual 8-chapter book. Here, every page has a skill or two, complete with the importance of such skill as well as the lessons you can learn from them. At the end of the chapter, there will be questions and a reflection section to help you express your thoughts and get the learning process started. In this book, the skills covered are separated into six categories:

- thinking skills
- communication skills
- emotional skills
- personal skills
- household skills
- financial skills

It's normal to be anxious about becoming an adult and gaining independence. Troubles at home, stress, hormones, and even the state of the world can make us feel isolated. Having a deep feeling that no one understands you makes the universe a much scarier place to navigate.

If you feel like you might not have what it takes to survive adulthood without relying on your parents, know that you are not alone! Even your parents might fear this for you because the world is filled with many endless possibilities, many of which are out of our control. Preparing for your future is the best way to maintain power over your life and where you're headed.

As a parent of two teenage twins of my own, I know what it means to raise teenagers, and I understand the ups and downs that you go through on a daily basis. Not only did I live through it myself, but now I'm relearning about the teenage experience through a new lens as I help my kids. What has made the biggest difference in our lives is the system of support, patience, and understanding we've built together.

This has inspired me to help share what we've learned along the way so that you feel less alone in your life's journey.

1

THINKING SKILLS

> *The essence of the independent mind lies not in what it thinks, but in how it thinks.*
>
> — CHRISTOPHER HITCHENS

Would you rather have to give up tacos or ice cream forever? If you had to evacuate your house in five minutes, what three things would you grab? Who is the person that makes you laugh the most?

Making decisions isn't easy. Each time we do, we go through a quick process in our brain involving critical thinking, reason, and past experiences to help us pick the best solutions.

Every problem can be solved first in our mind; you have to come up with a plan and a set of actionable steps to reach your resolution. Navigating this process involves a specific set of skills, and if those are lacking, it will be hard to reach your desired outcome.

THINKING OUTSIDE OF THE BOX

No matter what situation you find yourself in, having the ability to think your way out of it is a helpful tool. "Creative thinking" is a powerful skill that will enable you to adapt no matter what changes arise. This skill allows you to explore your imagination and express divergent thinking (Sigworth, 2020).

As you navigate through the education system, you will likely use creative thinking frequently. Whether it's a school project or a group collaboration, thinking outside the box can help you get your tasks done more efficiently.

Creative thinking skills will also be required in your career. Even if you are not following a creative career path or something involving the arts, you can still twist the perspective of a problem you're tackling to see it in a fresh new way.

Creative thinking helps you change your perspective. To start thinking a little bit more creatively, take a situation and look at it through a brand-new lens. If you are fighting with a friend, think about what a third person's perspective on your fight might look like. How would a narrator describe this scene?

This might not feel like creative thinking; however, it's opening a new part of your mind so that you can view a situation as it is if you're having trouble changing your perspective.

Ask somebody else. You can practice this by observing a piece of art and seeing the different ways that two people interpret it. Try watching a movie with a friend and discussing it afterward. What things did you both take away that were different? Creative thinking also involves crafting stories behind what you are working with. If you are trying to come up with a story, think about the background of the characters. What have they lived through that helped shape them into the people they are today?

When you apply reason to creative thinking, you allow your brain to think more critically.

THE POWER OF REASON

If everyone in the world had strong critical thinking skills, this place we call home would look a lot different. Critical thinking is important as it helps you:

- evaluate ideas.
- synthesize information.
- find connections and links between ideas and information (Sigworth, 2020).

Critical thinking allows us to evaluate misinformation so that we are able to form our own opinions and criticisms. Being able to see all angles of every part of a concept allows you to see the full picture. This is very useful in many areas of life.

As you likely already know, the state of politics today is a very heated topic. It's important to form your own strong political opinions. Everyone is entitled to their own belief, but what you choose to value should be strong and backed up with research and critical thinking skills.

Even if you believe you have a solid value system, take it a step further. Try looking at opposing viewpoints to the things you value, even in areas outside of politics. Flipping the switch and seeing things from another person's perspective combined with research will help give you the full picture of reality.

Critical thinking is important for something like choosing where to live. You can determine all outcomes so that you can be confident in the decision you're making. What are all the costs going to be? What are all the benefits? What are you going to gain from this decision?

Think logically and try to make decisions based on reason. Emotion will always help sway you when it comes to making a final choice, and sometimes you have to just trust your gut. However, research and reason will enable you to make sure that you are making well-informed and backed-up choices.

MAKING THE RIGHT CHOICES

How many times have you had this conversation:

- Person 1: What do you want to do?
- Person 2: I don't care; what do you want to do?

This is usually followed by a few more exchanges of "I'm down for whatever" or "I'm open." It's great to be easygoing and willing to try any experience. However, at some point, decisions have to be made. Voicing your opinion is hard because it means potential blowback. What if you pick the restaurant that gives everyone food poisoning? What if you pick out a movie that ends up being terrible?

When making the right decisions, it's crucial to follow a choice you are confident you can handle the outcome of. Don't let the fear of chance encounters keep you from trying new things and choosing what feels best for you.

All good decisions begin by weighing out the pros and cons. Writing down a list of both is proven to help make the decision process more effective (Morin, 2021).

Think of all of the options when making a decision, even obvious things. Write them down and take a day to look them over if it's a big decision. You might be missing something or you might not be viewing the entire picture.

Look at every sacrifice and every cost that it's going to take in order for you to get to the right decision. Is there a way you can choose both things you're split between by compromising something?

Think about who else is affected by the choice. If you're making a decision for yourself, it's important to follow what you want to do. However, is there going to be any outcome or downfall associated with this choice? Look at your reasoning behind why you're considering different options. Is there pressure from outside sources, or is this something that you are doing completely on your own?

IF THERE'S A PROBLEM, THERE'S A SOLUTION!

Everyone has problems. They are inevitable, but they don't have to be life-ruining. Developing problem-solving skills is important because research shows being able to solve problems and make decisions can lead to more success in life (Welker, n.d.).

Problems can be hard to solve because the first sign that there is an issue can become overwhelming in itself. All of a sudden, something bad has happened, so it's hard not to think about everything else that could still go wrong.

If there's a problem, remember to stop and breathe and start to think about what the core of the issue is here.

If you walk into the kitchen, open the fridge, and see that somebody has eaten your leftovers, you might get extremely frustrated with this person and scream, causing an even bigger fight.

Even if it was just a slice of pizza, you might get incredibly angry. What's the core of the problem here? It might not be that you don't necessarily have the pizza, but maybe you're not feeling respected by the other people in the house.

Create a plan A, B, and C to fix the problem. If you're ready for anything to happen, it will give you more confidence to take the next step and try to fix an issue. For example, maybe you're afraid you failed a recent test. Plan A can be to talk to the teacher and see if there is any bonus work you can do to keep your grade from dropping. If they say no, Plan B can be to put more effort into the class to ensure that you excel in the next few assignments. If you are still struggling and both plans don't work out, you can consider hiring a tutor.

Sometimes finding the right solution to a problem means just trusting your gut and knowing when to speak your mind.

SPEAK YOUR MIND

The driving force behind our actions is our thoughts. Behind our thoughts is our belief system based on what we're taught and the experiences we've had. Forming a strong system of values and beliefs helps to bring together all of the decision-making and problem-solving skills we've discussed.

This next skill is focused on forming your own opinion. There is so much influential media that we consume on a daily basis, not to mention the pressure from friends and family can make us feel like we should think a certain way. Your opinions represent your unique viewpoint and differing thoughts, so having opinions, owning them, and sharing them with others can help you strengthen your voice and connect to other people.

Know that you do not have to know everything. It's okay not to have an opinion on some things. You can wait and see how you feel. Sometimes perspective can only be shaped over time.

If two friends are fighting with each other and have completely opposite opinions, they might come to you and ask who you side with. The pressure to pick sides can be overwhelming, especially if you fear they might get mad at you. However, it's fine for you to work on your own opinion and see how things work out over time. You can stay neutral if you struggle to form an opinion and ask questions to get a bigger picture.

What is keeping you from being certain about one idea or the other? What are you apprehensive about? Follow your gut and learn to trust your intuition. Sometimes things simply will not feel right, and it's okay to decide to change your mind or not to have an answer.

Once you do establish a strong opinion, it's important to stand up for it. Though it can be scary to share, you might find that other people actually feel the same as you; they were just afraid to be the first to say it. Don't be afraid to share your ideas and stand up for who you truly are.

CHAPTER 1 REFLECTION

In each chapter, there will be a reflection section to help you review what you have learned. The more you focus your mindset on these life skills, the more they will become a natural part of your life and thought process.

Journaling is something that can be done in many different ways. You can use a physical notebook or journal to write in daily. Alternatively, you could use a notes app on your phone to keep track of your thoughts. Choose whichever method will make you the most comfortable so you can easily stay consistent with journaling.

Start each journal entry by answering these two questions:

- What lesson stood out the most?
- What is the importance of learning these skills?

Reinforcing information you just learned can help you retain it better.

Journal/Activities

For the first journal exercise, begin by writing down your goals for the future. Think about:

1. What goals do you have for your career?
2. What do you hope to be doing in the future?
3. What are you afraid of missing out on?

For the second exercise, write about the things that you want to learn. Where are you lacking the most skills? How has this negatively impacted your life?

Finally, write about what you are already good at doing. Do you keep your room clean? Is your homework always done on time? Do you do well at your after-school job or other extracurricular activities? Recognizing the things you are good at will make it easier to find confidence in your actions.

You don't have to write a response for each question; there's no deadline or length requirement. It's not homework, but instead, something that can help you reflect on your thoughts and get closer to achieving your goals.

Summary

If there's one thing to take away from Chapter 1, it's that you already have an endless amount of tools in your own mind.

You don't have to look outside of yourself for help; the best guidance will be your own internal voice. Finding and strengthening that voice involves reflecting on your choices, speaking your mind, and taking the initiative to find a solution.

One of the most important choices we will make is how to use our words.

Notes

2

COMMUNICATION SKILLS

> *Communication is the solvent of all problems and is the foundation for personal development.*
>
> — PETER SHEPHERD

Beyond your mind, the most powerful tools you will have in the future are your words. Communication happens daily. Exchanging phrases and expressions of language occur with yourself, your peers, your boss, and any other person you encounter. Many of us even talk to our plants and pets. You can't control what others say, but you're the only one in charge of the filter between what passes through your head and what is shared with those around you.

As a child, getting away with saying certain things was easier because you didn't know any better. As you age, that same courtesy isn't granted as often. In addition, you'll be more responsible for taking the initiative in getting what you want, and words will be very powerful in helping you to get there.

ON THE RIGHT PATH

Research shows that the way directions are followed can differ from person to person (Dunham et al., 2020). This depends on how the information is presented; the area in which the information is learned; and whether or not immediate action is taken after hearing the instructions or if that is something done later on (Dunham et al., 2020).

Knowing how to follow directions effectively can set you up with a life of success. The most obvious reason for wanting to follow directions is to ensure that there are no mistakes made. Beyond that, however, following directions is going to be incredibly important for you in school. Knowing how to pay attention and listen to what the teachers are sharing will ensure you get the best outcome from the assignments you complete.

You might find at some point in the future that you don't match the teaching style of one of your teachers or professors. Perhaps you are more of a visual learner, and they explain everything very factually on paper. If you understand how to follow directions, you can start to teach yourself what information is needed for an assignment as long as you stick to the requirements.

If this is the case, you can go home and watch videos and learn about the subject in a way that suits your personality and mindset so that you can still succeed.

Knowing how to follow directions ensures that you get the most from every learning experience that you go through. Check in to make sure you're on the right path so that you don't make things worse for yourself after making mistakes by not following directions.

BECOMING A SOCIAL BUTTERFLY

Social skills are vital for all ages, but the sooner you learn how to become a social butterfly, the earlier you will start to make connections. You never know who might be able to help you in the future, so it's good to maintain relationships. Social skills include things like:

- starting conversations.
- meeting new people.
- good sportsmanship.
- handling bullying (Lake, 2018).

Not everyone is a natural extrovert, and spending time alone or being shy might feel natural to you. That's perfectly fine! We all have different preferences. However, when the time comes, it's important to know how to interact effectively with others. In addition, you don't want to get used to being alone too much, as social isolation can become very lonely, especially if it causes you to lose relationships.

It's scary to put yourself out there and meet new people, but if you learn how to take the initiative and introduce yourself to others at a young age, it will only get easier over time. Other people can seem scary, especially if you're somebody who struggles with social anxiety. In reality, a lot of people are just as afraid as you are of meeting new people and having conversations with strangers.

If you can form a network and maintain social relationships, it will help you build a team of support. You'll be able to have people you can ask for help or others you can collaborate with for future projects. Ensure that you maintain these relationships as well. Sometimes simply checking in or calling them on the phone is enough to stay in touch with old friends.

TALK THE TALK

Words express ideas, desires, needs, and wants between two people. Knowing effective communication skills ensures that you can do these things with ease. Even in times of conflict, if you can share whatever you are feeling or thinking in a way that doesn't hurt someone else, you can find a solution.

Conversations can start with one person simply asking a question. If you introduce yourself to new people, you can ask everybody where they're from. If you are meeting up with future roommates before you go off to college, you can get to know them by inquiring further about their background. In some social situations, you might find that people don't really want to talk about themselves. Instead, you can focus on your own stories and background. Eventually, this might help the other person open up so that a flowing conversation can begin.

Focusing on yourself is also an important communication skill when you might find that you're in the middle of a conflict with somebody else. Share "I feel" statements and focus on the things that you are feeling rather than blaming the other person.

Never name-call or raise your voice when talking to somebody, even if you're upset. It can only make things worse and will put up barriers between the channel of communication that you and the other person have.

Never try to control somebody with your words. You can always express your opinions and share your feelings, but trying to withhold information or slightly changing facts in order to get the outcome you want can be manipulative behavior and is very damaging to relationships.

When communication is not happening properly, sometimes the best option is to take some time and walk away. Eventually, you will be able to come back together and work things out when emotions have settled. One of the most important parts of developing good communication skills is knowing how to be a good listener.

LISTENING TO UNDERSTAND

Equally as important as communication skills when talking to others are listening skills. Poor communication occurs when one person doesn't try to listen and instead uses the time another person is talking to plan what they are going to say next.

Listening to others is important because it:

- strengthens relationships.
- ensures accurate information is shared.
- creates stronger understanding.
- increases problem-solving and conflict resolution (Schilling, 2012).

When you are listening to somebody else, the first thing to remember is to listen without judgment. Try to control the way that your face might be reacting and nod along and pay attention so that they are comfortable with sharing things with you. Even if it's somebody telling you things that are upsetting or hurtful to you, reacting immediately can sometimes make them afraid to share even more.

Try to breathe deeply and listen to everything that they're saying, and give them a chance to share what is on their mind. If you grant them this courtesy, they're more likely to do the same to you when it's your turn to talk.

Hear what they are actually saying and look at the deeper meaning behind their words. Sometimes when people are listening to others, it's not to understand but to instead plan their attack. Don't listen to somebody else and just cherry-pick what you hear in order to suit your argument. Instead, look at the motive or intention for what they're sharing because this will help you resolve a ton of conflict in the future.

NO MAN IS AN ISLAND

Over the years, as your freedom increases, you might begin to feel this pressure to be as independent as possible. That's great! You should strive to flex your autonomy. At the same time, it's just as important to know when to ask for help. You might fear asking for help because it makes you look weak or inept. "No man is an island" refers to how no one can be that independent, no matter how self-sufficient they might look.

A lot of people your age won't ask for help because they fear that they aren't going to get the help that they're looking for. It can be very scary to know whether or not you can trust somebody, especially when you have been judged about your feelings already in the past.

Many people don't like admitting they need help because they don't want to feel helpless. They want to feel like they're in control.

Admitting that you don't have all the answers to a solution can be very scary because it can make you even more fearful of the outcome. Remember that needing to ask for help is actually a strength. Not a lot of people are able to have the courage to admit that they can't do it all and that they need somebody else's help.

It's not a failure of who you are. Instead, it shows that you are intelligent enough to know your skills and to know your own boundaries.

If you are ever afraid that you are going to get in trouble, do not let this stop you from asking for help. For example, if you have been exhibiting risky behavior or partaking in dangerous activities, and you need help getting out of these situations, please talk to your parents, a teacher, or somebody who can help you. Even if you get in trouble, whatever punishment you receive is going to be a lot better than the potential outcomes that risky behavior can have. Accept any consequences that you are afraid of happening now rather than waiting for things to hit rock bottom. In most cases, you aren't even going to get in as much trouble as you think because adults just want to help and make sure that you are safe, healthy, and happy.

THE BODY TALKS

Beyond words, bodies express most of what we feel. If you have the skill of reading body language, you will be able to find a deeper meaning behind what others are sharing. On top of that, you can see the true message of what others are feeling if their words don't quite match.

One of the easiest body signals to read is signs of nervousness. Think about how your peers look when they're giving speeches or presentations. Are they swaying, fidgeting, or talking fast? Sometimes shaking legs or wandering eyes can also indicate nervousness.

Signs of frustration might include rolling their eyes or throwing their head back in a deep sigh. Sometimes people fidget because they are nervous, bored, or it's simply a habit. However, look at someone's face and listen to their words when trying to dig deeper into what they are thinking or feeling.

Match other people's body language when you want them to feel closer to you. It can show an unspoken form of connection during a conversation.

Pay attention to where their eyes are looking. If someone keeps checking the clock, they might feel rushed or hurried. Are they looking around for the bathroom or a drink of water?

Help to open others up with your own body language. Sit back and open your arms, relaxing into your seat. You might notice the person across from you doing the same. If someone is feeling nervous, hand them something to help distract them, like a glass of water.

RESPECT MATTERS

Everyone deserves respect. Even if you feel disrespected by someone else, you can still choose to show them courtesy. Oftentimes, people refer to this as "being the bigger person."

One of the most effective ways to show respect to others is by choosing the correct tone of voice. It can help you gain attention, inspire others, and captivate audiences (Harappa, 2020).

Even if you're frustrated, you can check your tone and say how you feel in a nice way. Sometimes all it takes is a sassy tone to get somebody really worked up, which can create angry conflict. Be calm and peaceful because even if the other person is acting irrationally, you are doing your best to show respect, making your argument or your side of the story more valid.

Aside from conflict, remember as a general rule to give people their space and privacy. Don't walk into somebody else's bedroom, especially if the door is closed tightly; always knock and wait for a response. When you start living with other people, especially roommates in shared apartments, you are going to want to be respectful of each other's space. Make sure that you clean up after yourself and that they don't have to deal with your messes. Consider how your actions affect other people.

Understand that other people have their own perspectives and their own viewpoints based on their own experiences, so even if they don't align with your own or you disagree with them, try to remain respectful so that the same is granted to you.

CHAPTER 2 REFLECTION

Remember to reflect on these two questions:

- What lesson stood out the most?
- What is the importance of learning these skills?

Journal/Activities

For the first entry, ask yourself, what is a time that you can remember when your words were powerful?

It doesn't matter if they were used to hurt someone else, inspire someone else, or simply relay important information. Reflect on this moment to help you connect to the importance of your words. What was the long-lasting effect? What would you change about what was said?

For the next activity, think of a simple phrase like "How has your day been?" Try to say this phrase with five different vocal tones:

1. Angry
2. Excited
3. Sassy
4. Bored
5. Scared

After doing the activity, you will see that it's not necessarily what you said that mattered, but how you said it. Recognizing this difference is important when choosing how you communicate with others.

For the final activity, watch an episode of your favorite TV show on silent. What do you notice about their body language? How are they expressing their thoughts and feelings through the way their face and body move? What is the spacing like between them and others? Recognizing the body language of other people can help you gain a sense of how you're using your own.

Summary

Like a tool, your words can be used to either build something amazing or they can be incredibly destructive. A screwdriver can be used to strengthen a structure, or it can be used to take it apart.

Words should never be used against someone or to hurt others; in every situation, try to see how your words can be used to help fulfill the main purpose of why you're sharing them. Are you angry at someone else? Use your communication tools to express emotion and build a stronger bond between you and the other person rather than using them to cause damage and make things worse.

It's not the tool that matters, but instead, how it is used.

Notes

3

EMOTIONAL SKILLS

> *Use pain as a stepping stone, not a campground.*
>
> — ALAN COHEN

Everyone you know has emotions. They're feeling them right now! Emotions describe our mood, thoughts, and state of mind at any given time. They can exist on a spectrum from good to bad, with many people usually seeking certain emotions while trying to avoid others.

A lot of emotions can be both good and bad. For example, nervousness is sometimes positive; you might feel nervous before a date or a vacation. It can also feel negative. You might feel nervous when feeling sick or after hearing bad news.

Emotions can be incredibly confusing, and sometimes it's hard to identify which one you're feeling, let alone try to share those emotions with others in a way they understand. While even experienced adults struggle with their emotions, understanding how to manage them as a teen will help you learn valuable lessons about your feelings.

NO MORE EXCUSES!

In life, you will have endless excuses. If we were all granted $1.00 per excuse, we could be millionaires by now. Excuses are what we tell ourselves and others to justify our behavior.

It's important to know that having an excuse doesn't mean your situation isn't valid. If you're genuinely sick for the day, you can skip class or call off work not just for your health but to avoid the risk of spreading contamination.

The problem comes when there are a lot of "flimsy" excuses that don't necessarily warrant a reason that we can't do something. For example, cloudy skies could be a reason to avoid going for a run because you don't want to slip and fall in the rain. However, it's not actually raining yet, so you could try a quick walk around the block and hurry home if it does start to rain.

To avoid letting excuses stop you from getting things done, consider how genuine the excuse is. Did you think of it after you had already decided not to do something? Or did the reason you can't follow through arise naturally?

Seek the reason for the excuse to understand why it's there in the first place. Are you afraid of failing? Are you worried about the outcome? Are you simply not interested in following through with the task?

Excuses are also created when we struggle to turn an idea into action. Wanting to change your style, learn a new instrument, or write a book are all grand ideas and good goals to have. However, it's easy to fantasize about how great life would be in these situations. Creating an excuse is much easier than turning that vision into a reality, so be honest with yourself and avoid excuses.

MENTAL HEALTH, IT'S A THING

Most of us understand what our physical health means. It's a measure of how we feel, if our bodies are operating in the way they should, and what risks we present to certain diseases or illnesses.

Just as important is your mental health. This is a measure of your "emotional, psychological, and social well-being" (CDC, 2021). Everyone has ups and downs, so if you go through bouts of poor mental health, that's not necessarily the same as having a mental illness (CDC, 2021).

However, both can have negative effects on your body. Increased anxiety can cause aches and pains, and depression can lead us to ignore our self-care. Knowing the difference between poor mental health and mental illness is important to ensure you take the necessary steps when you find yourself in either situation.

Sometimes, you might find that you're not quite happy with how you look, which could lead to bad habits and some unhealthy choices. Most people experience this type of poor mental health at some point or another. Eventually, you might be able to pull yourself out of a rut and begin exercising and eating healthy to feel better.

Periods of poor mental health can come after a breakup, death, experiencing bad grades, or getting fired from a job. If you are experiencing poor mental health, it's helpful to first look at your habits. Are you eating meals with healthy fats, protein, vitamins, and nutrients three times a day? Are you getting up and brushing your teeth, grooming yourself, and getting dressed daily? Are you getting in at least a little body movement every day, like some light stretching or going for a walk? Try and turn these habits around if you find yourself in a mental rut. While it isn't always a direct cure, starting here can be a way to improve mental health on your own.

Having a mental illness looks much different than this, and it's important to understand the difference. Some people equate being depressed to having poor mental health, and while they can be similar, mental illness is more severe. Those who are clinically depressed or diagnosed with chronic anxiety might find they are completely ignoring their health, sleeping for long periods of time, and experiencing physical symptoms like nausea, racing heartbeat, insomnia, and various aches and pains. If you are unable to get out of bed and care for yourself, consider reaching out to your primary care physician and discuss your symptoms. Treating mental health can be much more difficult to fix on your own and might require therapy or medication. Remember, never be afraid to ask for help!

FROM OVERWHELMED TO EMPOWERED

When times of stress and anxiety arise, it can feel like the world is ending. If you learn the skill of stress management, you will be able to assure yourself that everything will be fine in the end.

Stressful situations are inevitable. What is currently stressing you out? Keeping up with your grades? Excelling in your extracurricular activities? Finding a place that you fit in?

As you get older, you are only going to have bigger decisions to make: What college should you go to, where should you live, and how are you going to pay for this? What career are you going to pick? What are you going to do after you graduate college? What are you going to do with the rest of your life?

Can you feel the stress mounting yet?

Now, what do you do to manage these feelings? Play video games? Hit the gym? Search for snacks?

Asking these kinds of questions can help you face stress head-on.

Stressful situations are never going to stop, but that doesn't mean you shouldn't try to find outlets to manage stress. The rain is going to pour; you don't have to get wet, you can use an umbrella.

Never ignore the problem. Pushing a stressor off means simply elongating when you have to deal with it. Things that are stressful do not simply go away.

Expose yourself to the stressor. For example, if the overwhelming pressure of college applications weighs heavily on you, start by simply filling out your name and address. All forms require this basic type of information, and simply opening the document and sitting in front of it can make it seem a little less scary.

FEELING ALONE... IT'S OKAY!

Everyone is alone from time to time; some people really enjoy this time, while others can't stand to not have social stimulation. Even if you thrive during alone time, too much loneliness has the same level of health damage as smoking almost a pack of cigarettes a day (Morin, 2023).

Loneliness is a feeling that will come and go over time. When you are feeling lonely, there are two ways to respond. First, consider if you are actually lonely or simply struggling to be alone. Everyone needs alone time to have moments of peace to reflect on their thoughts, reduce stimulation, and grow the inner bond they have with themselves. Feeling lonely can happen even when around others when we don't nurture that connection with ourselves.

Maintaining socialization is just as important as practicing alone time. If you get too used to being alone, that's all you'll ever want to do, and that can start to impact the way that you feel.

Join clubs with people who have similar activities, even if that means finding something online. If you live in a less populated area, finding large groups of people might be difficult, so use the internet to your advantage to further your interests and connections. Most importantly, connecting to others will help you when you aren't feeling like your best self.

IT'S OKAY TO NOT BE OKAY

Your emotions are important. Sometimes they are scary and figuring out what they mean takes practice. Improving emotional management means fine-tuning the skill of expressing your feelings.

It's important to learn how to sit with all of your emotions. Accept them for what they are. They make you human. They help motivate you. They help you figure out a deeper understanding of who you are as a person. Emotions are chemical reactions, and sometimes they can compound or pile on top of each other. If you find yourself feeling a negative emotion, more bad feelings can follow, such as guilt. For example, your friend might tell you they won a scholarship you had also applied for but didn't get. It's normal to feel jealous in this situation because you had wanted that for yourself. Not only might you feel bad because you're feeling envious, but you might also make yourself feel worse for not being a supportive or excited friend.

It's okay when you have bad feelings. Though sometimes emotions are referred to as "positive" or "negative," that doesn't mean you are wrong for feeling them. More people are struggling than you think and just aren't showing it on the outside.

Express your feelings to make yourself feel validated, understood, and heard. Sometimes saying things out loud or writing your feelings down can help you make better sense of what is happening in your head (*Expressing Your Feelings*, n.d.).

BE TRUE, BE YOU

There is only one you, and there will only ever be this version. All the chemicals in your brain that make you emotional, independent, and unique are individual to you and everything you've been through.

This unique person deserves to be shared with the world! Authenticity is an important skill to practice. Not only can it help you stick out from the crowd, but copying others can be illegal or get you in trouble, like plagiarizing.

The pressure to fulfill an image that has been created by others sticks with you into adulthood. What it means to be a perfect student, worker, or spouse looks different for everyone. Trying to copy someone else's version will cause you to lose sight of yourself and the things that you believe. Not only that, but trying to put on a fake persona just to appease others can be very tiring!

To practice more authenticity, look at the reasons that make you want to conform. Is it pressure from friends or family? Did you see something on TV that made you question a part of yourself? Don't let others define you; one opinion doesn't create global truth.

Reflect on your thoughts more and notice where they came from and why they're there. Sometimes you will realize that these judgments don't matter anymore.

Find safety within yourself. When you are honest and truthful about who you are, it will feel more natural to act on your gut feelings. The more you stray from who you are, the harder it will be to reconnect with yourself in the future.

Follow what makes you feel comfortable. If you are similar to others, it doesn't mean you aren't being true to yourself. Humans like a lot of the same things! For example, you might have the same style as your friends, or maybe you all share the same favorite band. As long as you are making this decision on your own, you don't have to change it just because it matches someone else. Look for other ways you are unique, and you will still find true authenticity.

LET IT OUT!

One good rule of thumb to follow is to never suppress emotions. They won't go away; they will only grow and get worse as you ignore them. One day, you will burst without warning, and it can make things even worse than when you first suppressed that feeling.

Think of it like a broken ankle. If you try to keep walking on it and don't go to the doctor, it will heal incorrectly and lead to many other health issues. Not only would you be in pain the entire time, but it would cause more pain later on when having to get surgery to try and fix the double damage.

Emotional expression begins with yourself. Stop and feel that emotion. Not all feelings need to be expressed; sometimes, you simply need to talk it out with yourself.

Consider if your emotion needs to be shared with someone else to fix a problem. Did a friend's actions make you feel hurt? Did your sibling yell at you and make you angry? Talking out your emotions can help you make sense of what you feel while potentially repairing relationships.

When taking steps to let it out, consider the best outlet. Are you artistic? Painting, drawing, or singing can be very emotionally expressive. Some people like expressing their feelings by working out to release anger and stress. Find an outlet that works for you and stick to it so that you are one step ahead of your feelings.

HEART AND MIND

A more advanced skill for you to practice in your adolescence is the use of emotional intelligence. You've likely heard of what an IQ is before, which stands for intelligence quotient. This is a measure of your thinking, reasoning, and information-processing skills. Your EQ is a measure of your social skills and ability to handle emotional situations (*Emotional Health*, n.d.).

There are four parts of emotional intelligence (EQ):

1. Being aware of emotions
2. Understanding others
3. Managing reactions
4. Controlling your mood (*Emotional Health*, n.d.)

Awareness around emotions is built by noticing what is coming in and out of your mind. Take it a step further and find a label or word that can represent your emotion. If you are feeling angry, you can pinpoint what type of anger that is. Are you frustrated? Are you filled with rage? Are you jealous? Are you feeling left out?

The second part is understanding the emotions of others. Once you have a grasp of your own feelings, it's easier to recognize how other people are feeling, and this will help you create stronger connections and improve your conversation skills because you can adapt to their emotions.

Once you are able to be aware of your emotions, you can manage your reactions. If you're feeling extremely angry, you can walk into the other room and count to ten as you calm down, rather than breaking things around you and punching the wall.

These three parts come together so that you can control your mood and make yourself feel better rather than having to depend on outside sources for emotional management. Your emotional intelligence grows over time, so getting to know what your feelings are will help provide the tools to build a high EQ.

FEELING FEELINGS

An emotion is a reaction, response, or feeling you have. An emotion involves three things:

1. Subjective experience
2. Physiological response
3. Behavioral or expressive response (Cherry, 2022)

Knowing how to deal with types of emotions and allowing yourself to feel the things you feel is a vital skill for people of all ages.

Part of identifying your emotions means understanding how those actually physically feel. Think about these situations and how your body might react:

- seeing your crush hold hands with a person other than you
- your shoe making a squeaky noise and the entire class thinks you passed gas
- your parents telling you you're grounded and can't go to your friends' party

In the first situation, you might feel sadness run through your chest. Perhaps your throat closes up, and you feel the urge to cry.

In the second situation, you might feel your face turn red, and all the blood leave your body as you sit there like a ghost, wishing you could turn back time.

In the third situation, you might start to breathe heavier, crossing your arms and stomping your feet.

Identify what it means to actually feel your feelings, and this will help you in future situations because sometimes you won't be able to pinpoint exactly how you feel in your mind, but your body will certainly tell you.

HEALING FROM THE HURT

Forgiveness is something that will change meanings to you over time. What does forgiveness look like to you now?

As kids, it was often us apologizing for an obvious thing we did wrong, and our parents usually told us, "It's okay."

As we get older, apologies and forgiveness look different for everyone. You're never too early to know how to forgive and determine what that looks like to you.

When you are ready to move past anger over a situation, it's time for forgiveness (Mayo Clinic, 2022). That doesn't mean the hurt or pain is gone, but it's a sign that you are ready to let the past become the past and create a different future.

Forgiveness can help you more than the other person.

When you forgive others, you are simply wiping your hands clean and moving on from the situation. How you decide to forgive and what the rules are after you forgive somebody is completely up to you. It could improve your health if you decide to forgive, as holding on to emotions can be damaging.

Forgiveness doesn't mean that the other person gets to hurt you again. You don't have to reconcile with a person that you forgave, either. Forgiveness is simply recognizing that you have a better understanding of the situation and you are ready to move on so that it no longer takes away from your present life.

EMBRACING YOUR AWESOMENESS

When was the last time you said, "I love myself?" You might say today, or perhaps you've never said this before. It can feel conceited to admit that you love yourself. However, developing self-love can improve well-being and increase confidence.

Practicing self-love at an early age can help you develop a strong voice. This voice can keep you confident and provide reassurance in tough times.

You can develop self-love by practicing saying nice things to yourself. If you are working on an art project and make a mistake, you might tell yourself, "Ugh, I'm so stupid." Instead, say, "No, I'm not stupid. I simply made a mistake, and I'm smart enough to know how to move on from that." Turn your negative thoughts into encouraging phrases. It will feel awkward at first, but eventually, self-compassion will come naturally.

Comparing yourself to others can damage your self-image, so be cautious about doing this. You never know what somebody else's situation might look like; everything could look perfect to you on the outside when in reality, they are struggling in ways that you can't even comprehend. When you compare yourself, you're insulting the current version of yourself.

Challenge the thoughts that you have—is what you were saying true, or is it simply an idea that was put into your head by somebody else?

Identify the triggering factors that make it difficult for you to love yourself. Often our peers and parents can contribute to the voice inside our minds. For example, if you are in the locker room after gym class, some of your classmates might look in the mirror and criticize their bodies. Somebody who has a smaller frame than you might say that they are unhappy with how overweight they are. It could make you feel bad since you feel you are larger than them. This can be damaging to our self-esteem even when they didn't mean to hurt us. Look at where their thoughts of insecurity are coming from. Remember that it is not a reflection of who you are but rather how they think (*Self-Esteem*, 2022).

COUNT YOUR BLESSINGS

Now more than ever before, it's easier to compare our lives to other people's. At any given moment, you can log onto social media and see people who have more money than you spend on things that you can't afford. Seeing things others have that we don't can make our lives feel empty.

If you are working two jobs while going to school and barely getting enough sleep, it's exhausting to get online and see that somebody who is your age is funding their own vacations, starting a family, or buying a house.

One practice that can help get you through moments when you feel like you don't have a lot in your life is gratitude. Gratitude is counting your blessings. It's not necessarily a religious practice; it simply recognizes all of the amazing things that you have in your life. Even if you could count 50 terrible things in your life, there has to be at least one thing that you have that someone else would be grateful for.

It's easy to start feeling down in the dumps and to blame yourself for the things that you don't have when in reality, other people just have luck. The person you see on vacation might have a lot of debt they used to pay for that. Someone who has a nice car might have wealthy parents. It's not your fault you don't have the same things, but constant comparison can lead to self-blame.

Start practicing gratitude every morning. When you're brushing your teeth, think of three things you are grateful for. Go through different categories. Start with your body. Do you have two legs that you can walk on every day? Do you have two arms that can feed you? Do you have the ability to see or hear? Of course, if you don't have these things, that doesn't mean you have nothing to be grateful for. However, we often forget to be appreciative of our own abilities and the level of our health.

Second, look at where you live. Do you have running water? Do you have a heater or an air conditioner? Do you have a bed with pillows and blankets? Do you have a couch and a TV that you can watch? Do you have a fridge filled with food? Do you have somebody that you love that you live with?

Take a look at your intelligence. Are you able to read? Can you do basic addition? Are you able to have access to the internet so that you can improve your intelligence? Are you able to write and form sentences? Again, if you don't have these things, that's not something to feel bad about. However, if you do have them, it's certainly a long list of things to be grateful for.

WALK IN THEIR SHOES

Think back on the tips we've discussed so far. How you feel your emotions, use your brain, and experience life can shape your perspective. The most important thing to know about perspective is that everyone's point of view is different (Johnson, 2019). How people act is based on their perspective, and that will change over time or fluctuate in different situations. Two perspectives can be true at the same time, regardless of the intention of the situation. Ultimately, no matter how hard you try, some people will simply never see your perspective (Johnson, 2019).

The best thing you can do for the peace of your own mind is to accept that everybody's point of view is going to be different. Trying to shape someone else's mind and see your perspective is exhausting if they view things in an opposite way. While sharing your perspective is wonderful, sometimes we have to simply accept to agree to disagree.

Do your best to see somebody else's perspective based on the information that is provided. For example, if your friend is being extremely mean to you and really short-tempered, think about what they might be going through. Are they struggling at home? What somebody is going through is never ever an excuse for how they get to treat other people.

If your friend is being rude to you, you should stick up for yourself and remind them that you don't deserve to be treated this way. That being said, a friend who is mean to you for a short period of time because they're going through something terrible isn't necessarily a bad friend. Alternatively, if a friend is mean to you every single time you hang out with them, and everything is going great in their lives, it might be a sign they aren't a great friend. Looking at somebody else's perspective can help you work through conflicts you have with other people, as perspective can drastically change a situation.

SPEAK YOUR TRUTH

Many of us are lucky enough to have a system of support and people to back us up. Even if you are one of the lucky ones, you might not always have someone with you when your strong voice is needed. Knowing how to speak your truth and stand up for yourself is a very important skill to practice as you grow older.

First and foremost, know your rights. You are entitled to your own opinion. You are entitled to your own beliefs. You are allowed to say how you feel and share your thoughts.

At the same time, you have to remember that your words are not free from consequences. You might say something that upsets others, and the result could be that they also share their thoughts. While you might feel like you're being silenced, in reality, they are simply expressing the same freedom that you have.

When you speak your truth, focus on your own feelings. Focus on your own thoughts. Speaking the truth can be very scary, especially in times of conflict. If you need to, ask for a moment so that you can collect your thoughts and write things down if needed.

If you have to share your truth with somebody in person, you can bring notes to help you keep sight and not lose track of what you are saying.

Remember that no matter what is happening, you always have the right to say "No," if somebody wants to force you to do something you don't feel comfortable with. You don't have to have a reason, excuse, or apology. You deserve compassion in any situation, so remember this when speaking your truth.

ONE COMPASSIONATE ACT AT A TIME

Studies show time and again that being kind is good for your health (*Kindness Matters Guide*, n.d.). Standing up for yourself means being kind to yourself, and that same courtesy should be granted to others.

If you think about it, kindness is respect and gratitude combined. It can be hard to give that effort to strangers, especially in our online world. Seeing such opposing viewpoints and violence in the news can make other people seem scary and aggressive. Practicing kindness can help you feel better and create a more positive perspective on others. It can improve social skills and decrease feelings of stress (*Kindness Matters Guide*, n.d.).

While you might not have a lot to give others, one thing you likely can share is your time. Giving just one hour a week as a volunteer will not only look good on your resume, but it can make a difference in the community. If we all volunteered for one hour a week, the world would look a lot different than what it does today.

Remember that when you volunteer your time to anyone, whether it's an organization or a friend, don't expect anything in return. Not everything has to be exchanged at a 1:1 ratio.

Beyond humans, be kind to nature. Always recycle. Littering is not just terrible because of what it does to the earth, but it also makes you look bad. If you get in trouble for littering, that could negatively impact your future or reputation. Some places are very serious and strict about littering, so never risk it.

Hold on to your garbage and always find a trash can or recycle bin. Recycle when you can, even if it's not offered in your building or your area. At the very least, you can find locations to drop off certain recyclable materials like cardboard, paper, or aluminum cans.

Spread kindness by sharing gratitude with somebody else. Tell a friend, parent, or sibling all the things that you're grateful for. It never hurts to do this. We often wait until Mother's Day or Father's Day to share with our parents how much we love them, but you can tell them what you're grateful for every day. Not only will it help them feel better, but it will act as a reminder to you why you are so grateful to be accepted and loved by these people in your life.

TOLERATING REJECTION

Rejection stings. Not getting the part you auditioned for, getting stood up on a date, or receiving a rejection letter from the college of your dreams can hit us in the gut. Why does rejection hurt so much? Rejection can be painful because it is the opposite feeling of one of our greatest desires—acceptance (*Rejection and How to Handle it*, n.d.).

Fear of rejection holds us back, so it's important to understand how to overcome that apprehension.

When getting rejected, remember that it's not a rejection from everybody. If a girl turns you down after you ask her out on a date, you might feel like all women hate you and that you'll never find a partner. This is not the case. You have no idea what somebody else is going through or why they might have rejected you. For example, that girl who turned you down might be going through a terrible breakup with her boyfriend. She might still have feelings and not want to move on yet. Perhaps she has to move away in a couple of months and is afraid to get close to someone new. There are a million reasons why you might get rejected, so remember that it's simply one situation and not a definitive truth about who you are.

Don't attack the rejecter; rejection is a visceral emotion, and you might want to turn that feeling right back around to the other person. Avoid doing this because it's only going to make you feel even guiltier later on.

Accept the criticism that might come along with rejection. If you end up not getting a job after your manager tells you that you aren't a great fit—reflect on your behavior. What could you have done differently? Usually, you'll find a morsel of truth in there.

All in all, rejection will lead you exactly where you're supposed to be. Ten girls might reject you, but one day you'll find the one who you love more than anybody else. You might not get that scholarship you worked for, but maybe you'll apply for a different one that's even higher and get that one. You never know what the future holds, so take rejection with stride and learn for the future.

SUPPORT, NOT PRESSURE

Fear of rejection can lead us to follow the crowd and give in to the pressure of peers. Handling peer pressure is one thing you'll likely have to face as a teen. When everyone else is participating in something around you, it can feel more validating to do the same. Peer pressure looks obvious in some situations, like teens offering you drugs or alcohol. It can also cause you to choose a certain university, dress in a specific style, or pretend to have an interest in things that you don't actually like.

To prepare for moments of peer pressure, know how you might react to different situations. If somebody offers you drugs at a party, what would you say? If a friend tells you that they can have their older sibling buy you alcohol, what would you say? If the crush you've had for months suddenly pressures you into taking your relationship further, and you aren't ready, what are you going to say?

It's important to have a visualization of these situations so that your morals and your ethics can remain strong under pressure.

Once those situations arise, it might be a lot harder for you to actually follow through with your desired outcome. Just like we discussed in the section on voicing your opinion, remember that once you take a stand, other people might follow, and they might agree with you. If one friend is telling a group of five to go to a party and sneak out of the house, everyone might follow because they don't want to be the one to say, "No."

No matter how much someone is pressuring you, you never need an excuse to say, "No." If a romantic partner is pressuring you into taking a romantic relationship further and you turn them down, they might start asking you really intense questions, like "Don't you love me?" or, "What, do you think I'm ugly?"

Though neither of those things is true, you simply might not know why you aren't ready to take the next step, and that's fine! You don't have to have an excuse. If somebody can't respect your "No," then they certainly are not worth your "Yes."

MIND OVER MATTER

Can you think of a time that you had no control and were free to do whatever you pleased? Maybe your parents let you eat ice cream for dinner, or you spent an entire day playing video games. When we have freedom, it's easy to take advantage of that time for all it's worth.

As you get older, having self-control is important so you can stay focused on what matters most. Improving self-discipline will make it easier for you to study for important tests, pay attention in class, and give all your attention to the things that deserve it the most. The level of self-control you have in adolescence correlates to the amount of self-control you have as an adult (Young, 2020).

Improving self-control means understanding the things that are taking your focus away. What are these distractions? For example, if you are working really hard to improve your strength, and you want to go to the gym after school every day, what is stopping you from doing that? Do you have friends who are always hanging out and encouraging you to skip workouts? You can have a talk with them and tell them that you would rather hang out later in the night after you get your workout in.

To improve focus, give yourself a reward at the end. If you're studying for a big test, it might be challenging to pay attention because you don't really see the immediate reward. Of course, having good grades is wonderful. But that doesn't seem like that big of a deal when you're sitting there bored, reading the same sentence over and over again while you hear your family laugh in the other room.

Have a reward for yourself. If you get an hour of studying done, maybe you can go join in on the festivities. If you get all your work done, you can treat yourself by going out to eat. Having a reward helps you improve your focus.

Most importantly, remember that breaks are important. While it might seem counterintuitive to get work done, sometimes walking away and taking a breather is the best method for you to come back and have a higher level of self-control.

PRACTICING MINDFULNESS

One of the most effective ways to have self-control is through practicing mindfulness. When you find your mind starts to float away, you can reel it back in through mindfulness. Thousands of thoughts pass through your mind every day, so it's normal that you will start to lose focus from time to time.

To begin practicing mindfulness, simply scan your surroundings, starting from the floor to the ceiling. Notice everything: How many walls are there? What's the furniture like? What objects are in the room? Now pay attention to your senses. What do you see? What do you smell? What do you taste and what do you hear? Simply doing this activity can keep you mindful in the moment.

You might find yourself spiraling in your head and thinking of all these anxious thoughts that only make you feel even worse. It's easy to start imagining fake scenarios of potential disasters and other bad outcomes. The potential of the future is endless, so you will always be able to think up a scary situation to make you stressed out. Mindfulness will help your mind say, "Stop, listen, and focus. This is reality. This is what's going on and you don't have to worry about the potential of the future. The only thing you have to do is focus on the moment right now."

To further the practice of mindfulness, consider having a mindful object. Use a small stone or coin and keep it in your pocket. When you feel anxious or nervous and struggle to focus, you can grab this mindfulness object and remain grounded. It will pull your thoughts back to a place where you are able to manage all of the ideas passing through your head so that they don't become scary scenarios. Remember that you don't have to finish a thought. Sometimes it can feel abrupt to go from a stream of thoughts into mindfulness, but that's just your brain still running off anxiety. Focus on the now and stay mindful. Practice this every day, and as much as possible, so that you can truly soak up the most from each and every moment.

CHAPTER 3 REFLECTION

There's a good chance that after reading about the last few skills, you already feel like you have a better sense of your emotions. There will be days when you might not be so sure, which is why journaling can be helpful. It's a practice of putting your thoughts into real words, making communication with yourself and others all the more efficient.

Reflect on these questions:

- What lesson stood out the most?
- What is the importance of learning these skills?

Journal/Activities

For the first journal activity, try free-writing about how you've been feeling lately. Set a timer for five minutes and write everything that comes out. Don't worry about making it sound perfect or using correct grammar and punctuation. Write out what comes to you, and reflect on these words after.

The next activity involves practicing mindfulness. You can try it right now! Identify all the things around you that are pink. How many items do you see that have more than two colors? What objects around you are made from wood? What is the most expensive item you see? What about the most valuable in terms not related to money? Taking time to create awareness of your surroundings can help you regain emotional control and feel better.

Finally, journal or reflect on how you handle different emotions. What do you struggle with the most? Some have difficulty with anger, while others constantly feel anxiety. Do you have any habits or patterns surrounding these emotions? Staying mindful of what we feel and how we cope with those emotions will ensure that we stay on the right track and don't fall into bad habits.

Summary

The older you get, the more you will learn about yourself. Staying in touch with your feelings can ensure emotional stability as you age. When you are in charge of your thoughts, you're less likely to give into emotional behavior like withdrawal, rage, and impulsivity. Stay mindful of not just your feelings but those of others, as this will help you gain a better understanding of emotions in general.

Notes

SHARING THE SKILLS

"We grow neither better nor worse as we get old, but more like ourselves."

— MAY LAMBERTON BECKER

Nearly everyone your age feels anxious about growing up and leaving home... But I bet you've rarely (if ever) talked about this fear with your friends.

It's common to think that you're the only one feeling this way. How is it that people just know how to be adults when you can barely get the duvet cover on without getting tangled up and turning yourself into a bed linen ghost?

Okay, maybe you're great at changing the sheets... But I bet there's at least one thing you struggle with that makes you wonder how you're going to tackle adult life.

How do I know this? Because it happens to everyone.

Yet it's not something we talk about... We're expected to ride the wave until we figure it out.

I wrote this book so you don't have to do that – so that you can learn all the essentials to adulting and make sure you arrive in adulthood fully prepared.

Now I'd like to ask you a favor… You can help me reach more people like you and make them realize they're not alone. Don't worry – it won't take you more than a few minutes.

By leaving a review of this book on Amazon, you'll show other young people that others share their anxiety about growing up… and you'll point them in the direction of all the information they need to know to ease their minds.

Simply by letting other readers know how this book has helped you and what they'll find inside it, you'll show them that there's help – and hope – out there.

Thank you so much for helping me to spread the word. I only wish I'd had this kind of information available to me when I was younger… and I bet your parents do too!

Scan Me

4

PERSONAL SKILLS

> *We are all self-made, but only the successful will admit it.*
>
> — EARL NIGHTINGALE

One thing you will learn as an adult is that many people are simply doing their best. We are all trying to be good partners, parents, and workers. We all want to achieve our goals and to do so in an easy way without a lot of bumps on the road. What you will also learn is that this version of "doing your best" looks different for everyone you meet.

We all have different ideas about how certain things should be done. Getting older means figuring out what the version of your best self looks like. This involves fine-tuning your personal skills. If you can master these things, your talent will trickle into all other areas of your life.

THE POWER OF NOT GIVING UP

There's a good chance you've already had a moment of struggling with procrastination in your lifetime. "I'll do that tomorrow" might be a common phrase in your personal dictionary. The best way to combat the desire to procrastinate is by cultivating self-motivation.

Starting a project is hard and giving up is easy. To help you avoid this, start by creating small goals and break things down into as little parts as possible. For example, if you're finding it difficult to stay focused on a test, you might just say, "Who cares? It's one test. I'm not going to study. I don't feel like doing this."

Instead, break it up into small pieces. Don't expect to have to read 50 pages in one night to study for the test. Start by reading just two pages. What is your worst subject? Where do you struggle most? Start there and focus on reading through these things. Even if you only study for 20 minutes, you might find that you at least get a C on the test rather than failing it completely.

Remember that mistakes are valuable. Don't give up because you're afraid of messing up. When you fail to act on something, that in itself becomes a failure. You may as well try, as a mistake can be seen as a free lesson.

FOCUSING ON YOURSELF

All day long, we run into people who think differently than we do. Trying to figure out what others are thinking or feeling can be impossible. What's important to do in any situation is to focus on yourself. What are you currently feeling? Does that need to be shared with someone else?

As children, there were five ways that we became aware of ourselves as separate beings (Cherry, 2023):

- differentiation
- situation
- identification
- permanence
- self-consciousness

Focusing on yourself means understanding what's different about you. If you see a teammate struggling during a game, you might think, "Why can't they just try harder?" Your skills are based on many factors, so embrace those differences and understand that not everyone has those differences.

Keeping your mindset focused on your thoughts and actions will help you prevent comparison or getting involved when it's not necessary.

HEALTHY RELATIONSHIPS

Healthy relationships usually involve the people you're friends with as well as your family members. How do you interact? Do you like each other? Do you enjoy spending time with each other? Just because you are in close proximity to somebody does not mean you have a good relationship with them.

As you grow, an important skill to learn is how to be a good friend, and this involves being compassionate and understanding to another person. It means giving your time to them and showing that you care about what they have to say. Check in with your friends frequently and see how they are feeling.

You should never try to make a friend intentionally feel bad about themselves. Putting other people down will only drive them away. The same rules can apply to your family members. Sometimes you simply will not get along with certain people in your family, whether it's the uncle who visits every other Christmas or the sibling you have to see every single day. Remember to stay focused on yourself in situations where you don't necessarily get along very well with other people.

Relationships can be old or they can be new. Look for new friends. Reach out to people. Even if you have a lot of relationships already, that doesn't mean you don't have room for another friend in your life.

Relationships are all about give and take. Sometimes you need help from other people, and other times you need to be there for other people. If a relationship feels a little bit more one-sided, that can be a time to have a discussion with that person and work through whatever issues are causing the relationship to be imbalanced. One way to maintain a relationship and stay connected to other people is to understand the importance of talking on the phone.

HOW TO TALK ON THE PHONE

Talking on the phone can be scary. You don't have the other person in front of you, so it's harder to pick up on some of their cues. You don't know what they look like or whether or not they're judging what you're saying. To make it easier to talk on the phone, begin by practicing with your friends. FaceTime them or just chat while the two of you are walking to or from class. When it comes time to make those professional calls, you'll be more familiar with your voice and have a better understanding of how you need to enunciate and pronounce words.

When it comes time to make those important phone calls, create a script for professional calls. Don't be afraid of the other line. Most of the time, it's automated, or at least the first parts are pre-recorded.

Having a script gives you something to refer to. It's also important to have a pen and paper so that you can write things down. If you try to remember it all, you might hang up and realize that you forgot everything and only have to make another phone call.

When you are talking to the other person, ask them how they are doing first and then state your name. After that initial repertoire has been established, state your need specifically. Be polite and talk slowly. Be clear and take breaths in between words and sentences if needed. Turn down all the sounds around you so that you can focus on the conversation. Talking on the phone is a practice, so it will be awkward at first, but eventually, you will get the hang of it.

SETTING HEALTHY BOUNDARIES

Boundaries are the specific rules and limits you set for yourself and others. This involves how people treat you, what is discussed, and what behavior is acceptable. Boundaries help you maintain your own self-respect. It shows others what you allow in your life and what you stand for. For example, if you are always letting people make fun of you or lending out money and never getting paid back, it shows that you might not have very strong boundaries.

The first method of boundary setting can begin with your body; you are in control of who is allowed to touch you, hug you, or hold your hand. You can set these boundaries with people before it even happens. If your boundary is violated, do your best to say something and stand up for yourself so that the other person knows what behavior isn't allowed.

Setting time restraints is also a form of boundary-setting. If you don't want to spend your time gossiping about other people with your friends, you can let them know this. Tell them that you don't feel comfortable gossiping and you'd prefer to change the subject.

As a second example, if a friend is pressuring you to hang out when you would rather focus on getting homework done and studying, don't allow them to make you feel guilty, as you are in charge of how you spend your time. Once you establish a boundary, state it clearly and check in over time if you feel like it needs to be reiterated or if someone has disrespected your boundaries.

PROTECT YOURSELF

Self-defense is going to be prevalent as you grow older. As you go out and explore the world, you'll start to encounter more people and have a higher chance of finding yourself in a situation where you might need to defend yourself. Though you might feel brave and ready for anything, your age group can be a target to predators as your age group might be a little more vulnerable. Less life experience can open you up to potential threats.

Don't go anywhere alone, and if you are alone, make sure it is during the day. There are fewer people out at night, and it's harder to see when it gets dark, so this is a more vulnerable time for all ages. Have someone who can walk you to and from class and make sure you have a ride home figured out after a night out.

Don't wear headphones when you are walking alone, and don't look down at your phone. If you want to listen to music, try using just one headphone or keeping the volume down low so that you can remain aware of your surroundings.

Don't tell anyone where you live if they ask. For example, if you find yourself in an elevator and a stranger asks, "Do you live here?" use this opportunity to lie and say that you're just visiting. Say the same if your Uber or taxi driver asks the same question when outside your house.

Don't tell people what time it is if they ask when walking down the street. This can be a scam to get you to stop and talk with them, making it easier for them to manipulate you, corner you, or lead you away from a crowded area. They might also be asking to see where you put your phone away, whether you tuck it into your pocket or slip it into a bag, making it easier for themselves or a friend to snatch it when you're not looking.

Don't open the door for anyone and keep it locked at all times. If someone asks for help, call the police first and use your best judgment before opening the door. Sometimes this can be a tactic to get you to open the door, only to be ambushed by others hiding out of sight.

Of course, you can't live in fear of everyone. Sometimes people genuinely want to know what time it is, or they're just making small talk when giving you a ride home or in the elevator. You might find yourself with someone knocking on your door who genuinely needs help one day—being afraid of everyone can be exhausting. The important thing to remember is to be aware of your surroundings, develop a strong intuition, and know how to protect yourself in any situation (Roth, 2019).

TIME MANAGEMENT

Like money, time can be budgeted. Begin by figuring out how much time you have. For example, if class starts at 7:00 a.m. and ends at 3:00 p.m., then you know that you can't account for using up this time. That means you then have 3:00 p.m. until your bedtime at 10:00 p.m. as your free time.

In these seven hours, what are you going to do? Sports practice might take an hour, band practice might take another hour, and homework is two hours. That means you have three hours to have fun or fill your time with whatever you please.

The worst way to spend your time is by procrastinating—this is like building up financial debt. Get ahead whenever you can, and take advantage of moments when you have an extra minute or two.

Chunk your time together with short breaks in between. If you have a lot of work or studying to do, it can feel overwhelming to only have five hours of free time and know that four hours of that is going to have to be spent studying. Break it down into four sessions with 15-minute breaks in between. This will help you stay on track so that you can guarantee that you'll get some enjoyment throughout your day while keeping your mind fresh for studying.

Avoid multitasking. While it might seem like this is going to make you use your time better and have more control over getting tasks done, what it actually does is split your focus and can make each task longer to complete.

Always give yourself more time when scheduling rather than less. For example, if a task normally takes 45 minutes to complete, give yourself an hour to do this rather than trying to get it done quickly in 30 minutes. What happens then is you fall off track, and it messes up the rest of your schedule, causing you to panic and feel overwhelmed.

When creating a schedule and figuring out your time management skills, ensure that you allot time for adequate sleep.

BEING FLEXIBLE OR PATIENT

If you ask anyone older than you what they wish they knew when they were your age, there's a good chance they would tell you to worry less and slow down. Patience is a virtuous skill to add to your collection of talents.

Whether you're waiting in line at a coffee shop or expecting news in your email, patience is something that will help you more than anyone else. When we're feeling rushed and urged, it's easy to let annoyance and frustration grow, and this can turn into aggression.

Like kindness, patience is also proven to be good for your health (Newman, 2016). Those who exhibit patience are less depressed, have stronger coping skills, and are able to display higher levels of mindfulness and gratitude (Newman, 2016).

When you are grateful, kind, and patient, you can display flexibility in any setting. Life will be filled with fun adventures, and when you open yourself up to sudden change, it will make things a lot easier for you in the long run.

While you might feel like time is being wasted, it will feel more fleeting if you spend time before and after being angry. Sometimes things just take a while, and there's no one to blame, yet feelings of anger during impatient moments can cause us to cast blame on our surroundings.

Display empathy in the situation. Whether it's a waiter running a little slow or a team member not as skillful as the rest of the team, be kind in these moments. Is there any way you can help? If your teammate struggles to catch the ball in a baseball game, what tips can you give them to improve? If a waiter struggles to keep up in a busy restaurant, be kind to make their night a little easier. A little patience can go a long way.

ALLOTTING TIME FOR ADEQUATE SLEEP

If you are 12 years or younger, you need 9 to 12 hours of sleep every single night. If you are 13 to 18, you need 8 to 10 hours of sleep a night. Anything older than that should strive to get 7 to 8 hours a night (Suni, 2023).

Your body is still developing and your brain is still growing. Your mind is shaping you into the person that you are going to be as an adult.

Sleep is required to make sure that not only does your brain get proper rest, but your entire body does, and this will help your health overall. Have you ever felt sick or queasy in the morning? Did you ever feel tired and like you couldn't stop yawning throughout the day? These types of feelings are very distracting, so getting the right amount of sleep is important to avoid allowing tiredness to take away from the day.

The amount of light around you can affect your sleep. Make sure you invest in some blackout curtains so you never have to worry about the sun waking up too early.

Avoid using electronics 30 minutes before bed since we are so sensitive to light. The light from our screen can make our brains think that it's still daytime, preventing us from getting to the right level of sleepiness needed before bed. Keep your phone away from you so that you are not tempted to look at it before you fall asleep at night.

Keeping your phone across the bedroom also makes it so that you have to actually get up out of bed to turn it off. Repeatedly hitting the snooze button can be bad for your health. Waking up and going back to sleep and waking up and going back to sleep multiple times within a short period can make you feel groggy and cranky throughout the day.

THE POWER OF YOUR CHOICE

You are going through such an exhilarating time right now because your choices are so powerful. While that can bring excitement about the future, it can also weigh heavily on you with fear if you are uncertain about what choices to make.

Recognize the power of your choice. Think of it like walking down a road. If you come to a fork, you can either go left or right. The paths can look similar for some choices, but for others, they are completely opposite. Sometimes those paths will come back together at some point down the line, but there's really no way of knowing. Think of the entire path of each choice when making a decision.

Choices don't arise just when presented with two options. We also have a choice for how much effort we put into things. We choose what we give our attention to. Know your limits and what things aren't a choice. Sometimes you have to simply walk down a path even though it doesn't feel great. Though no other paths are presented, you still have to take steps forward to get ahead.

Only you can make choices for yourself. Don't procrastinate decision-making because doing nothing is making a decision in itself. Usually, you suffer the most from the consequence of your choice or lack thereof. One thing that can make your choice stronger is to have a clear goal in mind.

SETTING GOALS

What does it mean to you to have a goal? Goals are important because they provide the framework for how we should spend our time, energy, and focus. Creating strong goals gives you the ability to look at a certain task or choice and figure out whether or not this aligns with what it takes to get the things you desire in life.

To set goals, the one effective technique to follow is the SMART method (Boys & Girls Clubs of America, 2022). This stands for:

- **s**pecific
- **m**easurable
- **a**ttainable
- **r**ealistic
- **t**ime-bound

Specific ensures you have practical methods to follow to get to where you want to be, rather than just floating through fantasies. For example, let's say you want to be an actor. Visualizing the glitz and glam of Hollywood is a nice way to pass the time, but what are the specific steps needed to get there? First, you might audition for the school play, and then you research the best places to study acting, and so on. These specific little steps help you to create the milestones to achieve your overall goal.

How can you measure your goal? In the acting example, you would measure this by whether or not you got the role. In another example, let's say you want to become the fastest swimmer on the team. You would measure this by recording your times and making comparisons to see how you've improved and how you can continue to improve.

Are these goals attainable? If you want to be a world-famous actor by the end of the year, that is a pretty high goal to try and achieve. While that could happen maybe years from now, rushing it can make you feel pressured and overwhelmed.

Are these goals realistic? Perhaps you want to shave a minute off your swim record. That is likely realistic to achieve maybe in a swim season, but not in a week.

Finally, find a way to time your goals so that you can make it easier to measure them while staying in line with your preferred milestones.

MOVE IT MOVE IT

As a teenager, exercise might remind you of gym class or competitive sports. Of course, there are exceptions, but many people either loved or hated gym class as a teen. Which category do you fall into?

The next skill to work on adding to your life is focusing on healthy movement. Adding in exercise isn't just important because of the reasons that we feel pressure surrounding it in school. Exercise is good for your cardiovascular system, can help manage stress, and it reduces your risk of getting certain diseases and illnesses (University of Rochester, n.d.).

Reset your mindset around exercise. Don't think of it just as a means to lose weight or make yourself a better competitor. Think about it as a way of nurturing and caring for your body. You don't have to look a certain way and you don't have to be the best at your chosen sport. However, you have to take care of your body because only you can do this.

Break it down into small sessions if you struggle to exercise (University of Rochester, n.d.). Teenagers need around 60 minutes of exercise a day. This doesn't have to happen all at once. You can work out in two 30-minute sessions or four 15-minute sessions. You could even work out in six 10-minute sessions or ten 6-minute sessions! Exercise can be running up and down the stairs a couple of times or simply walking a few laps around your dining room table. Little movements add up, so sneak exercise wherever you can.

Cardio is crucial for getting our blood pumping and working out our hearts. This is an exercise like walking, running, or swimming.

Strength training helps us build muscle, maintain stability, and increase coordination. This would involve using many weighted gym machines or using weights to do curls. It could also include using resistance bands or strength training exercises like pushups and squats.

Find a way to make exercising more fun, like creating a workout group. Watch your favorite show or play some music. Consider investing in small equipment, like a stair stepper or resistance bands. Use social media to your advantage to help you find workout videos. Exercise is a way to nurture your body, so it's a crucial skill to develop as a teen.

NURTURING YOUR BODY

Just like sleep and movement are needed for health, eating the right foods is just as important. All food is good food in that it nourishes our bodies. Avoid demonizing certain foods because that can create unhealthy relationships around guilt and shame, especially as a teen. What can help to differentiate between whether or not you eat something is the level that it is nourishing your body.

Be conscious of the way things are marketed toward teens. Sugary candy, coffee drinks, and fast food can become a part of our culture, and eating them in excess is normalized. Sure, a bowl of ice cream can nourish your soul, especially on a hot summer day. However, excessively eating ice cream every night might not be the most nourishing, depending on the amount and type.

Get three meals a day, and remember that they should be balanced and colorful and should include a protein, like meat or beans. In addition, include whole grains, like rice and pasta. Finally, use fruits, vegetables, and herbs to season meals and add extra nutrients.

Do your best to limit fried foods and sugar. They are inflammatory and make it difficult for our body to break them down.

While you might feel the urge to skip breakfast, especially if you're running late in the morning, do your best to eat at least a little something. This will kick-start digestion for the day and help you improve focus. While certain habits develop at home, ultimately, it's up to you to take action on your health and make the right decisions.

TAKING EFFECTIVE ACTION

Gaining independence and control over your future is all about having initiative, and this means taking action when it's required. Taking action means displaying grit, a combination of passion and persistence (Christian, 2020).

Stay strong when times get tough. No one is going to have more of an effect on what your future looks like than you. If you power through and you know how to face your problems head-on rather than running away from them, you'll have more control over your life. You'll be able to make better decisions for yourself, and you'll be less likely to run into issues. Don't rush through or take shortcuts, no matter what you commit to. Whether you agreed to babysit or you are studying for a test, it's important to stick to the plan, follow directions, and take action to accomplish that task.

Taking shortcuts can result in poor work quality, or it might make someone less likely to trust you and your authority. Have high standards for yourself and for others, and stick to them. Stay optimistic and encouraging, especially if you find yourself taking action in a position of leadership. For example, if you are a camp counselor and you are taking kids out on a field trip, have high standards for yourself for safety protocols.

Take action if you notice that somebody is being a little bit too unfocused when caring for children.

When the teacher asks who wants to go first when giving presentations, take action. If your boss needs someone to cover a shift, take action. If your parents struggle to keep up with chores because they're working two jobs, take action.

IT TAKES A VILLAGE

No man is an island, and it takes a village to make a community run smoothly. When you have the time and resources to do so, it's good to focus on giving back to the community. Volunteering your time can have benefits in your professional life, education, and personal life (Heldt, 2021). Having community service experience on a resume could increase your chance of landing a job by 27% (Heldt, 2021).

Connections, skills, and experience matter, and these can all be gained when you give back to your community. Think about letters of recommendation and experience on school applications and how much of a difference this can make.

Personally, you might meet new people that become lifelong friends. You can also gain experience and new perspectives on life different from yours. Most importantly, it's not about you but your community and giving back to help build a better future for everyone.

Think about what career you want and how you can volunteer in a related field. For example, if you want to become a kindergarten teacher, join a club catered towards young children. If you want to become a nurse, see if there are clinics you can help volunteer for. Donating your time will also help you learn how to work with others and accept them without judgment.

ACCEPT WITHOUT JUDGMENT

Judgment is natural because we are wired to form conclusions, thoughts, and insights into people and the situation around us. Sometimes judgment is necessary, like if you're working late at night and a customer starts to make you feel uncomfortable. If they're giving off creepy vibes, you might press the panic button or call coworkers for help to ensure your safety.

Unfortunately, judgment can often become misguided. Sometimes judgments feel like they come naturally to us, but in reality, a lot of the criticisms that we have of other people are taught to us.

When you judge others, you're also creating standards for yourself. You're forming a list of rules that not only are you judging other people on but that you are going to hold against yourself. If you are judging the way that other people look because they have unkempt hair or clothes that are out of style, that puts more pressure on yourself. If you find that your hair doesn't look great one day, you're going to make yourself feel bad about that because you aren't living up to your own standards.

When you judge other people, you're judging the size of an iceberg based on just the tip. What you see on the surface is such a small percentage of what's actually going on. If somebody is not looking their best, maybe they don't feel very good. If somebody seems a little unfocused or scatterbrained, maybe there's something that's going on at home.

Instead of judging, ask where this criticism comes from and what purpose it serves.

Sometimes we have no choice but to make judgments. If you're choosing between two people you want to work on a team with, you are going to have to look at their past experiences and see if they are the best fit for the role. It's not always easy to make certain judgment calls but remember that you are a lot stronger than you think.

BEING RESPONSIBLE!

When thinking about responsibility, your mind might fill with homework, chores, and other daily duties that you have to do. While responsibility certainly includes rules that you should follow, it goes deeper than that. Break the word down:

Responsibility = response + ability

How able are you to respond to a certain situation? If it's your responsibility to make sure the dog gets taken out on a daily basis, you are responding to the dog's needs to use the bathroom and your household's needs to not have poop and pee ruin the floors. If you're responsible, you take the dog out several times a day as needed and clean up if there are accidents. If you are not responsible, you will ignore this duty and let the dog go where it pleases.

Failing your ability to respond will result in natural consequences. Going above and beyond will give you even better results. To practice more responsibility:

- Stick to a schedule and show up on time. Waiting until the last minute or allowing lateness to become the normal standard will weaken your ability to be responsible.

- Keep your area clean and tidy. Lockers, cars, bedrooms, and eventually dorms, homes, and apartments are our responsibility. You might have roommates, siblings, and eventually spouses/partners to help you clean, but you still have to do your fair share.
- Take the initiative to do things before someone else tells you to do them. This allows you to get ahead of tasks and have more control over the steps it takes to accomplish these things.

If you do mess up, take responsibility for that as well. Apologize, admit what the fault was, and agree to fulfill the needs required to overcome the situation.

STRONGER THAN YOU THINK

Think back to when you first learned to ride a bike. You were probably pretty scared during that first push that you didn't have the training wheels attached anymore. Feeling that balance deep in your stomach can be really scary, but you chose to keep going. Even though you could have stopped and let yourself fall over, you kept cycling and pushing your feet forward. Resilience means that you look failure, setbacks, and obstacles right in the face, and you decide to keep pushing through (APA, 2020).

As you're reading this, raise your hand as high as you can. Hold it for a second, and now reach even higher. There's a good chance that you had a little bit more height in you than what you had initially reached for.

You are a lot stronger than you think.

When the world is weighing heavily down on you, remember that you always have a little bit more to give. It's easy to let the world keep piling on top of us, and before you know it, you'll feel like you're too weak to push back. One bad day does not mean that you have a bad life. Keep focusing on taking the next step forward.

KNOWING YOUR CORE VALUES

One skill that makes resilience easier is knowing your core values.

The easiest way to understand core values is to think of what you were taught growing up about what it means to be "good" or "bad." This might be based on your religion. What have you been taught is right or wrong? What makes a good person versus what makes a bad person?

Values change over time, and they're also frequently tested. Knowing what your value system is makes your voice stronger. Values can change shape over time.

They can grow or shrink, and they can disappear altogether, only to be replaced by a value that is the exact opposite. Values aren't inherently good or bad. Someone might believe it's good to take what you want and focus only on yourself, while someone else believes you should care for others and always give.

Having strong values makes it easier to know who you are, what you think is the right thing to do, and what you should focus your time and energy toward. Think about the value system that exists between different religions. Does this play a role in your life? What about values regarding the law? Do you think that the law is just and ethical? Do you think that there are some things that could be changed in the government?

Values also involve work ethic, how we use money, and the views that we have about our health. Values go into creating our perspectives on love, compassion, and empathy. Your values will show how you lead others, as well as the amount of success you're able to achieve. Values also infiltrate friendships and other relationships. Look at the values that people in your life have, as well as what you already believe. Follow a path that allows you to be open-minded about how your values form over time (Selig, 2018).

STAY IN COURSE

Have you ever gone out to eat and ordered a dish, only to regret your decision after seeing the meal of your dinner guest? Maybe at the time, the pasta looked the best, but now that they have the sizzling sirloin, you can't help but think about how your own meal isn't up to par.

Committing to decisions can be incredibly challenging, especially in times when our choices fall flat. Commitment is based on:

- trust
- intent
- effort
- sacrifice (Pickhardt, 2014)

Making a commitment means making a promise about your future. A committed relationship means that you agree that you aren't going to see anybody else and that you're only going to focus on one person. Committing to a sport means that for an entire season, you are going to go to practice after school and games on the weekends. Committing as a teen can be hard because not only are you surrounded by a lot of influences, but your future's so unknown. You're still figuring out who you are. How can you commit to big things in life?

What if you don't do very well at your sport and you decide you want to quit? What if it's too much for you after trying a new activity in finding that you don't actually have the passion or energy to give to this? If you commit to something like cheerleading, it can be very expensive to pay for training, clothing, shoes, and travel to different competitions. Before committing to anything, consider all of these factors so that you can take a step forward without fear.

Once you make a commitment, it's always good to follow all the way through. Though you might feel like it's over and you just want to give up, try at least one more time. At the end of the day, follow your gut because you know what's best for you. But sometimes, you're going to have to push through that fear and stay true to your commitments.

UNDERSTANDING THE CHANGES IN YOUR BODY

Puberty can be a scary time in adolescence. Not only is your body changing, but the way you think might begin to shift. When your peers are also going through these changes, it can create new dynamics in friendship groups and cause conflicting emotions to arise.

Find peace in knowing that you are normal! These changes are common, even though it might not feel like that at the time you're going through them. Puberty can be an awkward subject, so even adults might avoid the topic. By understanding what changes you'll be going through, you can feel a little safer knowing that your body is normal.

First, you might notice changes in how you feel. What you might like, the things you find funny, and the people you enjoy hanging around might change during this time. Sometimes things might seem scary, but adults have been through it.

You might start to feel attraction toward others or want to explore different levels of relationships. Everyone's experience is different, so remember the skill of focusing on yourself when it seems like the world is spinning rapidly around you.

Your body hair, voice, and skin will go through changes. You might gain weight or grow in height. Reading about others' experiences and exploring this topic can help you feel less alone during such a pivotal time in your life.

PERSONAL GROOMING AND HYGIENE

Hygiene is important because:

- it can help prevent disease or infection.
- it can change how we appear to others.
- it can change how we smell and help alter body odor or bad breath.
- it can make us feel confident in ourselves.

Hygiene starts with bathing. Shower daily. Use soap on every part of your body, including behind your ears and under your armpits. Wash from top to bottom, and don't forget your feet. Use a separate cleanser for your face, especially if you struggle with acne. Your body produces sweat and sheds dead skin, and it's necessary to wash all of that off consistently. When you're around a lot of people at school and even touching others during practices, you never know what kind of bacteria can be transferred between two people.

You don't need to wash your hair every day. You can wash this 1-3 times a week or as needed.

Brush your teeth twice a day, once in the morning and once at night. Floss once a day, and avoid rinsing your mouth with just water after you brush to let the toothpaste sit on your teeth.

Keep your nails trimmed and clean, and avoid dry skin by using lotion and lip balm.

Use antiperspirant daily and after workouts. You might not smell it, but others do. Pair this with perfume or cologne, but only a spritz or two. If you can smell your own perfume or cologne, you might have sprayed too much.

Practice these things daily, not just for yourself but for those who will be around you. This is the first step to having good manners.

MANNERS MAKETH MAN

Good manners are some of the first words we learn as children. Saying "please," and "thank you" is an easy way to show appreciation to others. Good manners can take you a long way and will help you get ahead in life.

Manners leave a lasting impression (Sonnenberg, 2016). A simple "Thank you for your time" to the person giving you a job interview can help you stick out of the crowd. If you say good morning and goodbye to your bus driver or the lunch lady, they will take note.

Show courtesy and grace to everyone. Be respectful of all workers, and offer a smile when you can. Good manners make communication easier, and it can increase comfort in any situation.

There may be times when you'll have to fake manners, but this doesn't mean you're inauthentic. If you're at work and someone is being rude to you, sometimes it's easier to give a forced smile and apologize to help keep the situation peaceful.

Sometimes people act loud or rude as a way to establish control, but it doesn't do that. Acting in this way only makes others around you uncomfortable, even if they don't say that to you out loud.

You never want to ruin the relationship with bad manners because it's such a small thing to emulate. Manners show others the values you have, like gratitude, respect, and responsibility.

Leading with good manners can also help you avoid future regret. If you act rude impulsively, you might feel bad later and need to apologize. Having good manners can prevent this from happening so you can breeze through relationships with little conflict.

FINDING YOUR PASSION

School, career, and shared interests with friends are great, but what are you passionate about? What is something that you wake up thinking about? When you go to bed at night, what are you excited to do the next day?

It's normal not to have an answer for this; finding your passion can be complex. The best skill you can have for finding your passion is that of exploration.

To find your passion, start by exploring creative outlets. This is drawing or sketching. Do you like creating animations or comics? What about surrealist paintings? Consider crafts or woodworking.

You can also be passionate about physical hobbies. Do you enjoy skateboarding or dancing? Do you have a favorite sport?

Musical hobbies are next. This involves singing, playing an instrument, or collecting records, and it could also lead to a passion for other types of media, like movies or video games.

Hobbies can also be things you do at home, like cooking or gardening. Explore all of these things even if you haven't before. You might pick up a new hobby and realize it fills a part of you that has been missing for a while.

When you find your passion, you can apply that to your future. Do you want to become a chef? Would you rather go to business school to open a restaurant?

Take your passions further and consider adding a competitive aspect. If you love photography, you could enter a contest and submit your pictures.

Is there a way to make your passion a group activity? Adding friends and people with similar interests can make it more enjoyable (*Why Hobbies Are Important?*, 2019).

THE VALUE OF TEAMWORK

The most independent people have to work on a team at some point or another. During your summer job at the ice cream stand, you will likely have to work with 1-5 other people during a shift. If you're a lifeguard at a local pool, you'll need to know how to work with fellow guards to ensure the safety of the swimmers. During school projects and class lectures, knowing the dynamic of a team can help you communicate easier and collaborate in the most effective way possible. Even freelancers who work from home work in teams from time to time. If you choose a job in the medical field, collaboration will be necessary to help people survive!

To work effectively on a team, remember these important tips:

- Share your strengths and speak up on what your desired role would be. Share your talents so that you can ensure you and everyone else are assigned the best role based on their skills.
- Make feedback a normal part of communication. Discuss what you think might help others and be willing to take criticism in return.
- Create group goals together. If everyone agrees to a deadline, it can make you all more accountable for sticking to timelines.
- Leverage connections and help strengthen your team's power. If you're missing an element of the team, see if they have the resources to help fulfill your duty, and see if you can provide something in return.

LEADING OTHERS

Leadership skills are helpful in avoiding peer pressure, excelling in your education, and forming a strong voice (PennState Extension, n.d.). A leader is someone who has the knowledge to understand what the best decisions are, the courage to play any role, and the willpower to know when to make sacrifices and do what is right.

Once you are in a leadership position, first identify your responsibilities. Write these things down so you can refer back to them when you feel lost. These are the values of your role in that specific leadership position.

Be willing to learn. Being a leader isn't the exact same as having complete power. It's fine if you don't know everything and still need to ask for help or group guidance. It's better to ask for an opinion to make the right choice rather than trying to flex your ego and make a mistake for the group.

Show confidence without arrogance. Be brave without having to prove this courageousness by putting others down. Model the behavior you want as a leader, as those who are following view you as an example. What you do is what they are allowed to get away with, so act wisely in front of others.

Some leadership positions we seek out, and others we naturally fall into. If you are an older sibling or cousin, these younger kids look up to you. Set a good example.

STAY IN SCHOOL!

Think about your biggest icons. Who inspires you the most? Try and think of 10 people you look up to. How many of them stayed in school? Education is essential; it provides confidence to those who go to school, and it is a gateway to endless connections. You can make life-long friends at school while developing your mind.

When you attend school and dedicate yourself to your education, it provides assurance of your future. Those who don't graduate high school earn $200,000 less over their lifetime than those who did (*11 Facts About High School Dropout Rates*, n.d.).

Having a good education can increase many of the skills we've discussed, like critical thinking, getting in movement, gaining new perspectives, strengthening relationships, and managing emotions.

School takes you a step closer to your goals. It helps you figure out at an early age what you're good at with little risk—if you fail math in junior high, you know next year to start off stronger in your first class, no big deal. Even further, if it remains a constant struggle throughout high school, you know to avoid anything mathematical in your career.

While you might not be the next mathematician, or maybe you avoid the arts, you can take away from school what you need to help strengthen your passions and improve your skills.

HOMEWORK RESPONSIBILITIES

Reinforcing helps you remember things better and retain information (Darn, 2007). Even if you feel as though you have already learned the things your homework covers, reviewing this information will make you more likely to retain it.

Homework is a chance to work through what you're struggling with so that you can apply more effort toward that topic. If you run into issues at home, you can bring them up in class with the teacher. Chances are, other students have the same struggles, so everyone will learn better in this situation.

If you're struggling to follow along with homework, consider leveling it up. Take it to the library or coffee shop, and see if friends can help. This is a great way to make connections with friends as well. If you're struggling in class, turn to your lab partner or ask the person behind you if they would be willing to help you study. Create a group to help further connections and make studying even more exciting.

USE STANDARD SOFTWARE

Familiarizing yourself with how to use certain types of software helps you make the most out of the product, which could improve your productivity. It adds extra skills to your resume and could make homework easier.

Familiarize yourself with popular word processing programs like Microsoft Word and Google Docs.

Understanding how to use spreadsheets will also be very helpful. You can use these to organize your time and personal schedule while also having another useful skill to add to your resume.

Learn presentation software such as PowerPoint or Keynote. It can make school presentations more exciting. Utilize as many free tools and forms of software as you can, and practice with your own fun projects. This might be your daily routine, a goal list, or a mood board.

Whatever technical skills you practice will be very useful when it's time to find an appropriate job.

FINDING AN APPROPRIATE JOB

As a teen, the job you get now doesn't have to be the job you'll have forever, and chances are high that it won't be. That doesn't mean you can't still make the most out of a part-time or afterschool job. Find something that works with your strongest skills. Are you a people person with charisma? Do you like organizing and record-keeping?

Consider the easiest location closest to you as well. Can you get there on a bike? Take a walk in your area to find places that might be hiring.

When creating your resume, list out every skill that you have. Find a way to put a professional twist and choose your words carefully. For example, if you used to babysit on the weekends, you can state that you formed connections with customers, are CPR certified, and prepared and managed meals for 1–2 individuals at a time.

Read the job listing thoroughly and connect your skills to these duties. Bring these things up in an interview, and you're sure to land the job. As soon as you start working, you earn money. Next comes a valuable life lesson: learning the value of money. We'll be covering this in the next chapter.

HOW TO DRESS FOR SUCCESS

Having your own style is a big part of creating your identity. Whether you like wearing vintage band t-shirts and ripped jeans, or you'd prefer khakis and a polo, what you choose to wear says a lot about who you are.

While looks don't matter in terms of whether or not you're a good person with strong virtues, they can matter in the workplace. Depending on your school or major, it could be an important part of what you wear to class as well.

Stick to timeless classics. This includes black pants, khakis, or nice jeans for more casual professional settings (like working in a kitchen). Stick to white or blue collared shirts buttoned up.

Ensure comfort when working. While looking good is something to keep in mind, you also want to be able to focus. Pick black flats instead of your stiletto red bottoms.

Remember who you're representing when dressing. You might be representing your school, job, or simply yourself. Make the right choices to show a good representation.

Show personality in small ways. You don't have to feel like you're wearing a costume when dressing professionally. Try adding a pop of color to your tie or with a cardigan. Jewelry and cufflinks can also help you represent your personality. Stay modest—it can show respect to many people in professional settings.

DATE SAFELY!

Dating is a fun part of being a teen. The "crush" stage, butterflies, and first kiss are vital parts of teen romance. In this day and age, it's more important than ever before to be safe when dating. The world wide web provides endless ways for us to meet new people. As you gain independence, you gain the ability to explore the internet in your own way. However, the internet access you have is the same one that many dangerous people have access to. That's not to scare you away from dating forever! Follow these tips to make sure that you are safe from harm and can instead focus on building a special connection with someone who treats you with respect.

Meet outside and in a public area when going on a first date. Get there on your own and have a ride afterward. If they pick you up, they'll then know where you live. Having a ride home also ensures a backup plan if things go wrong.

Share where you will be, and a picture of what you're wearing wouldn't hurt either. Don't let this cause you to be paranoid; it's better to do this a bunch of times and have it not matter rather than not doing it when it could have saved your life.

Verify your date's identity and don't meet up with someone that you can't do at least a little research on. Do you need to look up your crush's aunt's Facebook to see what her dog's birthday is? Of course not. But if your date only has one profile picture and his page was made two months ago, he might not be real.

Be cautious if your date is forceful about these things. For example, if someone insists on meeting at their home late at night, that is a huge sign they are up to no good. Avoid recreational substances on dates, as they could alter your judgment, and if you do have a beverage, never, ever let it get out of your sight. Keep it right in front of you with your hand around it and on top (University of South Carolina, n.d.).

ROCK YOUR VOTE

Unless you are pursuing a career specifically in politics, your vote is one of the only ways you can make a difference in your government. Socially we can influence people and their beliefs, but submitting your ballot is one of the best ways to physically participate as a citizen during election time.

Registering to vote is very simple. The best way to do this is to go to usa.gov. There, you can register to vote. You also have the option to vote through the mail, which can make things even easier when it comes time for election day.

Check your mail consistently for information about upcoming elections, and do research on which candidates are running. Use the other skills we've discussed, like forming your own opinion, to make sure that your vote represents you in the best way possible.

Regardless of your political affiliation, it's your right to make your voice heard. When filling out ballots, you don't have to mark every category if you're unsure about smaller elections. You don't have to share with anyone who you voted for; just ensure that you're making a well-informed decision. The people you disagree with vote, and those you agree with also need help.

USING TECHNOLOGY

What separates a lot of generations is their relationship with technology. Those born in the sixties are likely familiar with smartphones and apps now, but if you hand them a video game console, they might get confused. Alternatively, toddlers who are barely walking can take pictures of themselves or choose what YouTube video to watch on their own.

Right now, you probably know more about technology than a lot of adults. While it seems like you have it figured out, things will rapidly change over the next decade, and the new generation will yet again have a different relationship with technology than you.

Keep your technological skills sharp. Even if you don't have a personal social media, familiarize yourself with what different apps there are. It can help you stay up to date with what is popular, which could help you find a way to leverage this to your advantage.

Take advantage of all the features that apps have. Research features they have that you might not have been aware of. Get to know creative apps for photo editing or video creation. Knowing some of these basic technological skills are great on your resume.

Technology can be beneficial to your hobby. Take these interests online so that you can find ways to make them even more enjoyable. There is so much free information on the internet. At the same time, it's important to check in with how much you're using the internet.

LIMITING SCREEN TIME

Though little is known about just how much technology affects our lives, studies seem to show a pattern: too much screen time can have damaging effects on our health. Some days you might check your phone first thing, get on the computer at school, and hop onto your gaming console when you get home. Technology isn't just used daily anymore—a lot of times, it's used all day long.

Not only is it vital to limit screen time for your health, but also for your attention. Activities that stray from the screen can increase your focus, improve sleep, and help you maintain a healthy weight (Mayo Clinic, 2021).

Read physical books to give your eyes a break from the screen. Books are a great way to entertain you while also helping to give your brain a workout. The same can be said for physical writing. If you have a paper due, try taking it offline and physically writing it out instead. To help you get into this habit, consider joining a book or writing club.

Spend time in nature. Even if you need to use a screen to study, you can at least take it outdoors so that your eyes can have a break in small intervals between study sessions.

Play board games and do puzzles with friends. Both can be inexpensive or found at thrift stores. Learn card games to play in groups. Schedule weekly sessions of playing a game or doing a puzzle. It might not seem like the most thrilling thing, but once you sit down and start laughing and chatting with your friends, you'll realize it's a great way to make the time pass while avoiding periods where everyone is sitting on their phones.

Reflect and listen to music or an audiobook. Though you might still be using an electronic to listen to these things, you can focus your eyes elsewhere to provide an opportunity for deeper mindfulness.

Try an artistic hobby like crocheting, knitting, or painting. Any form of craft is a great way to use your mind and hands without having both glued to an electronic. You don't have to demonize phones and technology in general, but limiting usage can help you regain focus and have better control over your attention.

SOCIAL MEDIA AWARENESS

Limiting screen time is important, but once you're actually online, it's crucial to create awareness about what and how you're using different apps and social media. Of course, apps like Instagram, Twitter, and

TikTok are great for staying connected not just to peers but to the culture of your generation in general. Social media can be addictive because it activates our reward response. Seeing notifications begin to buzz from likes and comments on a recent post can make you feel excited, validated, and happy. However, overuse of social media can lead to compulsions, making you feel the constant urge to check in with what's happening online. This can cause distraction from things that you should be focusing on, as well as increase feelings of anxiety when you're not able to check social media.

Avoid comparison and remember reality. It's very easy to photoshop your body to look different than it does in reality. Real bodies have hair, stretch marks, scars, bumps, and blemishes. Our weight and appearance can fluctuate, not to mention how much lighting and angles can alter the way someone looks.

Always be wary of who you're talking to, and like dating safely, make sure to verify their identity. While they might seem like a nice person, it's easy to steal photos of others and talk in a convincing way.

Keep your reputation safe. You never know what posts might pop back into your life years down the road. The things you say or do online could stay there forever, and you never know if future employers, partners, or other important people might get ahold of the regretful things you shared.

When you decide to post, limit the information you share and keep your location safe. Never share street names, license plates, or pictures/footage that make the outside of your home easily identifiable.

CHAPTER 4 REFLECTION

Everyone thinks and acts differently, and it's that very reason we are all unique individuals. Sometimes, however, our actions and thoughts can get in the way of us feeling "normal." Knowing how to complete these basic personal skills will help you breeze through life, even in times when you feel a little isolated from others. Reflect on:

- What lesson stood out the most?
- What is the importance of learning these skills?

Journal/Activities

To help you further reflect on the lessons learned in this chapter, go back to the lesson that stood out to you the most. Then, think of an example of when:

- you displayed this skill.
- you could have used this skill but didn't.
- you saw someone else use this skill.

For the next reflection activity, do a quick online search of open positions for your dream job in your desired area. If you want to move to New York to become a doctor, conduct a search there. What skills do they list? Do these line up with some of the things you've learned in this chapter? Do you have what it takes to eventually fulfill these skills? This might be a ways ahead, but it's always a good idea to know the types of personal skills that will be needed in your desired career field.

Finally, take some time to list out your responsibilities. What tasks are you in charge of? Are any of these shared with siblings or parents? Consider chores, homework, and keeping your room clean. Now, take some time to reflect on if you are doing a good job of taking responsibility for these things. If not, consider writing out some ways that you could improve.

Summary

No one is perfect! Our minds work in a way that makes us often look for methods of improvement, so it's good to focus on what successes you've had. Putting a strong foot forward and focusing on your values is the best that you can do.

Results will vary from time to time, but as long as you stay focused on what you want in life and take charge of who you are, most outcomes will be positive.

Notes

5

MONEY SKILLS

> *Never spend your money before you have it.*
>
> — THOMAS JEFFERSON

One of the most transformative relationships you will have over time is how you interact with money. Right now, money might be something meant for having fun, like buying food or going shopping. Plenty of kids your age are also already earning money for their families.

As an adult, money becomes your level of accessibility to many different things in life. The amount of money you make and how you choose to spend it will determine your home, car, and how you spend your free time. The sooner you learn how to manage your money, the more flexibility you will have with these things as you get older.

WHY SAVE YOUR MONEY?

Big purchases like your first home might seem far away. When you're a preteen or teenager, it's easy to spend frivolously since you might not have bills to pay. However, starting to save can set you up for a life of success, no matter what age you are.

Five dollars can have different values at different times in your life. If you're a kid in a candy store and someone hands you a $5.00 bill, you get to spend it excitedly. When you have a $1,200 house payment due, $5.00 doesn't seem like a lot. It's important to keep a perspective that you had as a child. $1.00 can go a long way! Putting just $1.00 in your savings account here and there can make a difference. One day you might simply need $20 to go on a date or see a movie with friends. Having that reassurance that you have at least a little something in your savings can increase confidence.

Over time, you can increase this amount. Try adding $10 every week or $50 a month. Some banks offer high interest on your savings account, meaning money that sits in the bank can earn a few extra dollars here and there.

In ten years, will you be happier that you spent your $500 paycheck on clothes that have gone out of style, or will you be happier that you saved it for the future? Of course, there's a line between being responsible and experiencing your life, so everyone deserves a treat here and there. You know what is best for your future, so do what you can to ensure that it's a positive one!

THE VALUE OF MONEY

Value of money changes over time. Today's U.S. dollar was worth $13.33 in 1920 (Webster, 2023). The value is only going to keep changing. The value of money for you personally changes based on your perspective.

The value of money is measured by time. If you work for $10.00 an hour, then a $50.00 concert ticket is five hours of your time.

Money can also have a higher value when it's invested or gaining interest, like in a savings account. Money that is tied up in debt has less value. For example, a $20,000 loan might become a $35,000 loan by the time you are able to pay it off, due to interest.

To reflect on this, what does money mean to you? Consider how different people you know also value money. Knowing the value of money will give you the skills needed to maintain financial self-discipline.

FINANCIAL SELF-DISCIPLINE

Making these smart financial decisions can be terrifying. The thrill of potential freedom and the excitement of new purchases is enticing. However, the more financially literate you are in adolescence, the likelier you are to find the same success as an adult.

One in two households is only "one emergency away from financial disaster" (Berman, 2013). There are many reasons why someone might be struggling financially, and sometimes there are factors outside of our control. That's why it's so important to save up when you can to prevent the consequences of these disasters.

Be mindful of why you are spending. Where is the pressure coming from? Take accountability for your financial habits. Take spending breaks and set goals to avoid spending any money for a certain period of time.

Keep your money out of sight to avoid the temptation of spending it. Instead of dining out with friends, consider buying ingredients instead to cook together. It can be a fun experience that saves all of you money.

HOW MUCH ARE THESE?

Knowing the basic cost of things can help you decipher whether you're getting a good deal or not, and this can help you make good financial decisions. If you're aware of the basic cost of things like milk, eggs, or bread, you can decipher if you're going to a store with prices marked up or if you've found a spot with great deals.

Focus on things that are on sale, and buy generic items to save money. Oftentimes, the same brands own generic companies, and in some cases, it's even the same product with a different label.

Things like household cleaners, razors, or paper towels are easily swapped for generic brands. Shampoo or skincare might be something you splurge on, but basic ingredients and household essentials are usually pretty standard.

Go grocery shopping with your parents and scan the prices. If you have an idea of what each ingredient costs, it will make it easier to plan low-cost meals.

Always compare prices online when making purchases. Check different stores because the same product made by the same company might have three different prices depending on where you choose to shop.

Beware of the green tax. Some products trick you into thinking they're better by using green labels and imagery of more "fresh" ingredients. In reality, a lot of companies know that you are willing to pay more if you perceive the object as "safer," so they charge more. When you familiarize yourself with the basic cost of things, you are taking one step ahead on the road to financial self-discipline.

BUDGETING BASICS

Budgeting means creating a plan for your money. Each paycheck or allowance, you are given a certain amount. If you break that amount down and allocate it to certain parts of your budget, you can ensure you're spending your money smartly.

One method to do this is the 50/30/20 rule. This means half of your income goes to the things you need. A third goes to the things you want, and the last part is for savings and debt (O'Shea et al., 2022). As an adolescent, there's a good chance you don't have a lot of needs or debts that your budget needs to be saved for. You can still use this formula to help keep your budget focused. If you have leftovers after fulfilling your needs, add them to your savings to help set you ahead.

EARNING AND MANAGING AN ALLOWANCE

Three in four teens are paid an allowance (Lake, 2022). Most parents set requirements for how this is earned, and the average allowance is just shy of $20 (Lake, 2022). This means that teens account for a lot of spending in the country! There are around 27 million adolescents in the U.S. (Begody, 2023). It's estimated that teens account for over $40 billion in spending every year (Begody, 2023).

Clothing companies, restaurants, and production companies know that there is a lot of money to be made from people your age. Advertisements work hard to make their products appealing because they know someone younger might be more prone to impulsive spending.

When choosing how to manage your allowance, consider splitting it into three categories:

- short-term expenses
- savings
- charity or gifts (Linwood, n.d.)

Since you might not be paying utility bills, like expenses for electricity, water, or gas, short-term expenses can be small costs you have. Perhaps you have a field trip with a fee or a birthday party and want some spending money. The first category can be for that. Next is savings, and finally, don't forget about setting aside money to give away. This helps you improve gratitude and practice kindness while reinforcing the value of a dollar.

SMART SPENDING

When it comes time to spend the short-term savings you acquired, it's crucial to make smart spending decisions. This is a skill that is hard to manage for a lot of people. Having extra cash can start to fulfill fantasies. New clothes can change your identity and fancy dinners can make you feel glamorous. However, living beyond your means and struggling to keep up with spending habits is not only stressful, but it can take away from your financial well-being in the future.

First thing's first: Consider earning more money if you want to spend more. Saving might seem like a difficult thing to do, and maybe your friends are always doing things that cost money. You're young, and you can take advantage of this freedom to spend a little more as long as you're making more. If your parents aren't giving you a high enough allowance for you to save some, consider getting a part-time job. Can you pick up a few more hours or an extra shift at your job? Perhaps you can find someone to babysit just once or twice a week. You have to spend at some point in your youth because you will get exhausted if you avoid fun altogether. However, it's also important to stay smart and spend your money in the right way.

Avoid social media pressure and the constant ads you receive. The job of advertisers and social media managers is to make sure that you spend your money. Many people are really good at their jobs, which presents a challenge to teens with disposable income.

Wait to spend money. If you see a shirt you have to have online, wait a couple of days before buying it. Don't fall for "limited availability," as fast sellouts are simply a marketing tactic to add urgency to spending. Wait at least 24 hours for purchases that you are unsure of.

Take the item somewhere else in the store when shopping in person. The store hires people specifically to design displays for the same reasons that social media managers work so hard to make their page enticing: they want you to spend money! If you see a display of luxury candles all aligned nicely with color-coordinated organization, it can make you want to buy that. Instead, take the candle away from the display and set it somewhere else to see if you actually want the single candle or if it was the display that was being sold to you.

Do a quick addition of the sum items before you checkout. Pull out your calculator and add everything together. Round up and don't forget about sales tax. For example, if you have things that are $1.27, $3.39, and $8.64 in your cart, round up to $2, $4, and $8. With tax, that'd be $15 rounded up. Are you okay with spending that much? If not, pick an item to put back. Spending smartly is the best way to avoid debt.

UNDERSTANDING CREDIT CARDS

A credit card can feel different from other debts because it's not granted for a specific purpose, like a house or car loan. A credit card is a personal type of loan that is granted to a person from a credit card company. There is a spending limit, from as little as $50 to $10,000. Of course, some are higher, but it will all depend on your credit score, which is covered in the next tip.

Credit cards can be taken out from different companies that exist specifically for lending. They can also be taken out at department and online stores. Banks also provide credit cards. When you apply, you will have to provide your income and usually a house or rent payment. Different factors can determine whether or not you are approved.

While at first, it can feel like free money, the catch is in the interest charged. The annual percentage rate, also known as APR, is the amount that you have to pay each year based on the debt owed. For example, if you received a $1,000 credit card limit and your APR is 25%, by the end of the year, you would pay $250 in fees and interest charges if you kept the card maxed out.

To avoid paying these fees, you can pay down the debt after spending. This is a good way to show future lenders that you are responsible with your money when they check your credit scores.

WHAT ARE CREDIT SCORES?

You're never too young to know what a credit score is. This is a number between 300–850. It's based on:

- number and amount of loans, credit cards, and other debts
- history of paying on time
- inquiries, which occur if you apply for a credit card or apartment/lease
- how much credit you have available (Opperman, n.d.)

Sometimes low scores occur even when you don't have any credit, as this shows you're not experienced with borrowing and making payments. Opening a credit card at a young age can help your credit, but it can just as easily lead to poor spending habits. It's tricky territory and is something to discuss with your parents or guardians. Never take out a credit card if you aren't able to make payments on it, as avoiding payments will damage your credit score.

When you miss payments, max out credit cards, and ignore lenders, your score plummets. This will make it hard to apply for an apartment, student loans, or car leases.

Having good credit shows lenders that you are reliable and that they can trust you with your money. Practicing good spending habits will help you improve your financial-making skills, setting you up for a flourishing financial future.

LEAVING A TIP

Tips are given to service workers. Some people tip based on service, though often, people stick to tipping at least 15% on services. Some of these services include:

- waiting/dining experiences
- deliveries
- haircut/dye
- transportation/taxi service
- cleaning services

Tipping isn't required, but it does show gratitude, courtesy, and kindness to those who provided you with a service. Some service workers make more of their money from tips than they do from their hourly wage. Though there is controversy over whether or not tipping culture is good or bad, there's no denying that it's not going to stop anytime soon.

Always tip 15% at the minimum, though when you feel the service has been excellent or the cost of the service/food was lower than the value gained, you can show extra appreciation with even more.

When you're in a pinch and trying to figure out the amount, move the decimal to the left one spot, and double that amount. There, you have 20%, which is a great tip. Use this example to help you become an expert tipper:

Let's say your bill is $25.00. Move the decimal to the left once. This gives you $2.500, or $2.50. Double that and you get $5.00. That would then make your bill an even $30.00.

AVOIDING DEBT

While you might gain access to credit cards, personal loans, and car leases over the next few years, it's still good to try and avoid as much debt as possible. One of your most valuable financial skills will be not spending money you don't have.

Pay off credit cards right away if you do ever take one out. A $100 purchase could quickly add up interest if you avoid paying it down for a while.

Create a savings account for a down payment on any debt you might accrue in the future, like if you need a car for work. You might be moving somewhere after college or starting a job that requires a vehicle, so you might not have a choice but to take out a car loan. The bigger the down payment, the better off you will be, so even though you might not be able to purchase a $20,000 car, you could lower payments with a $5,000 down payment.

Don't buy things you don't need with debt, like food and clothing. If you have to spend your credit card, it should be for life requirements, like school supplies or books. You might need to buy a bed if you're moving into an apartment, but buying a bunch of decorations isn't as necessary. Focus on needs only because going into high levels of debt cancels out any of the fun you had when making the initial purchases.

Pay your savings account as if it's its own bill. For example, you could schedule a monthly $25 transfer to your savings and simply pretend it's a bill that you need to pay. This can help you create strong savings with minimal effort.

Pay higher than the minimum payment on debts. If your credit card payment is $25 monthly, try to go for $50. It's okay if you have months where the minimum is all you can afford; however, when you have extra, put it towards your debt.

Cut up credit cards that are close to or at their limit to keep you from spending. You can save the pieces so if there's an emergency, you still have the card numbers, but this will prevent you from taking it to a store where you are more likely to spend impulsively (*How to Avoid Debt*, n.d.).

UNDERSTANDING STUDENT LOANS

Skillful spenders avoid debt; however, it might be the only option for some. If you are passionate about getting an education but have no money, nor do your parents, student loans might be your best option.

If taking out student loans for college, try to choose a major that is practical as you might not get a job right away, but the loan payments might start coming. For example, studying film is a great road to take if that's what you're passionate about! Consider minoring in education so that you can teach if needed. You might also minor in something technical, like software development. You can still follow your dreams of becoming a filmmaker, but this is a highly competitive field, so having a practical backup skill can help you find a job when you need to make ends meet.

Sometimes there is some leftover after your tuition is paid, which can be used on room and board, as well as supplies. This is called a "refund check." Though this can help struggling students, don't forget that this also needs to be paid back. For example, you might receive a $20,000 loan, and room and board is $15,000. You would then get a $5,000 refund check. You still have to pay the entire $20k plus interest.

You can pay for school with a combination of loans, grants, personal payments, and scholarships. There's not one singular way to pay. If your tuition is $15,000, you might be able to pay $1,000 with savings and $2,000 with money that was gifted to you during your graduation party. Then you receive a $4,000 grant, meaning you would only need an $8,000 loan.

Grants don't have to be paid back and are usually given to lower-income households. This will be based on your parent's income. Some careers will forgive loans if you work for a certain company or government facility, but there are specific rules in these types of situations. Applying for student loans is done by filling out a free application for federal student aid (FAFSA).

Loans are both federal and private. Private ones usually have higher interest rates and are less forgiving than government loans. While college is exciting, make sure you make the right choices (Ellis, 2022).

If you're really struggling financially, consider going to a university that is less expensive for the first two years while you work on your prerequisites. Then when you have to take more advanced courses, you can transfer to your preferred college.

LEARNING ABOUT TAXES

When you finally start to make your own money, there's an amazing feeling of empowerment when you get to cash that first check. After putting in long, hard hours on hot summer days, now is the time to put that sweet cheddar in the bank. All those long nights of smelling like grease while other kids your age were out partying have finally paid off.

That is until you see the breakdown of the taxes withheld. Seeing such a high percentage can be jarring, and everyone has a moment of, "Why do I have to pay taxes?"

Taxes pay for many government expenses as well as the well-being of our fellow citizens. Taxes also pay for wars, police gear, and the subsidization of animal products. Government workers, teachers, and libraries are all funded by taxes. We all have to pay for this, even if we don't agree with how it is spent.

Taxes are automatically taken out when you are employed, as the person employing you usually provides a W-2 when you start. This is usually for jobs that provide hourly wages or set salaries.

Some jobs are categorized as self-employed. These would be rideshare app drivers or food app delivery drivers. Dog walkers and babysitters might also be self-employed. In this case, workers are responsible for reporting their own income and paying an estimated quarterly tax.

There are many online sites that you can use to help you file taxes when that time comes. It can be complicated, so do your research before and ask for help for your first few years of filing.

GROWING YOUR MONEY

An investment is a way that you can spend your money to watch it grow. While it might sound like a perfect way to generate passive income, it also comes with risks. Some people make careers out of investments, while others use them to make a small stream of extra cash.

Popular types of investments include those in real estate, the stock market, or savings bonds. You can invest in future companies and receive revenue. You might invest in a rental property and receive income from tenants who pay rent. Alternatively, real estate investing is done when someone purchases a property, fixes it up, and then sells it for a profit. In some cases, real estate investors simply buy a property, sit on it for years as the neighborhood changes or property value increases, and then sell it once the value has risen.

It's a great way to make sure that your money safely grows. Investing in various assets helps to make sure you have multiple streams of income, ensuring less risk. This is known as "diversification."

As a teen, your best and safest option is to start small with a savings account. This way, you can set money aside and forget about it while you focus on your future, allowing you to draw from it down the line when you really need it and it has had time to grow. As your financial literacy grows, you can begin to research stocks and how to invest in these as a way to boost some of your income.

STASHING YOUR CASH

The safest way to make sure your money is secured is in an actual savings account with a bank. Keeping a safe or a jar hidden somewhere is great so that you have easy access to your money, but it can be risky. It's harder to keep track of, and if you live in a dorm or area where a lot of people might be coming and going, there's no way of knowing if it's totally secure.

When opening an account at a bank, you have a few options. You can open a checking account, savings account, or investment account (Rockwood, 2020). A checking account is the best form to start with. This will ensure you can set up direct deposit with a future job, or you can get a debit card to spend your funds immediately.

A savings account is a great thing to pair so that you can keep your money separate. A long-term savings or investment account is a third option for letting your money grow.

When you have a checking account, you have access to checks or debit cards. This is how your money will be withdrawn immediately. A deposit is when you put money into your account, and a withdrawal is when it gets taken out (Rockwood, 2020).

Learning all of these financial facts can feel overwhelming. You might not have any money at all, so all this talk of it could be stress-inducing. Don't panic! You have time to learn these things.

GETTING INSURED

Debts and loans are money you don't have that is given to you for certain reasons with the promise that you will pay it back. Debit cards and savings accounts are tools you can use to manage the money you do have.

What if you don't have money and an emergency arises? What if you get into a car accident and need auto repairs, or you break your arm and need to go to the hospital?

That's where insurance comes in. Insurance is money that is given to you only when it's needed. To have access to insurance, you normally have to pay a monthly fee.

Insurance is purchased most commonly for health, cars, and houses. Life insurance is also frequently purchased, which is a sum of money that is given to family members or other beneficiaries after a person dies.

Some health insurance is free, like Medicare or Medicaid. There is no free auto insurance, though it is legally required to drive in the U.S.

Much of the time, adolescents are able to be on their parent's health insurance and won't have to worry. Universities also often provide low-cost healthcare. If you're unsure of what healthcare you have now, ask your parents about what policy you are on and what coverage you have to get an idea of how it all works.

Even if you're incredibly healthy or believe you are the best driver on the road, insurance matters. What if someone else drove recklessly and hit you, causing an expensive hospital and mechanic bill? While you can be responsible, the same isn't guaranteed for other drivers on the road, so it's best to ensure you're safe with insurance (Dowshen, 2018).

CHAPTER 5 REFLECTION

Managing money starts by recognizing the way that you view it in your life. Money shouldn't be the only source of happiness, but pretending that money has no meaning can be irresponsible. Reflect on these questions:

- What lesson stood out the most?
- What is the importance of learning these skills?

Journal/Activities

For this journal activity, start by answering these three questions:

1. What is your current relationship with money?
2. What have you learned about money from how your family makes and spends it?
3. What have you learned about money from peers and media?

Writing this down will help you gain insight into what level of financial literacy you are at now. In the future, as your savings grow and you learn more responsibility with money, you can come back to this journal entry to see if your perspective has changed.

Depending on your age, the next activity can involve budgeting. If you have an allowance, savings, or income from a job, record how much money you have.

Next, write down all of your expenses. Do you have bills to pay? What purchases are you saving up for? Do you have any money you can put towards fun things and other activities? You can choose to spend your money in any way you choose, but practicing with a budget can help you gain more financial independence as you get older.

For the last activity, create a jar you can start saving extra cash in. If you have an actual savings account, deposit it at the end of the week. Practice saving the change after you get snacks with friends or even coins you find on the ground. Seeing how quickly a savings stash can grow will give you the confidence to make healthy financial decisions in the future.

For extra encouragement, decorate your jar with things you might want to buy in the future. For example, you could tape a picture of your favorite musician to it so you can buy concert tickets to eventually see them live.

Summary

Money isn't the key to happiness, but it does help speed things along on the road to success. When you're confident with your finances and making smart decisions for your future, it will ensure that you don't have to worry about money as much and can instead focus on other things that matter.

Now that you have learned about your emotions, personal skills, and how to manage your finances, it's time to use those smarts and apply them at home.

Notes

HOUSEHOLD SKILLS

> *Have a place for everything and keep the thing somewhere else. This is not advice, it is merely custom.*
>
> — MARK TWAIN

One of the greatest joys of young adulthood is having a home that you can call your own. When you have your own space, you get to follow your own rules. What's most important to remember about this, however, is that freedom brings out new responsibilities.

If you develop the following household skills while still living at home, it will be even easier to make them a part of your daily routine in the future. In addition, this last chapter will include some extra tips that will help further your independence.

FLEX YOUR REFLEXES

You're never too young to know how to react in an emergency. Whether it's a natural disaster, an accident, or a normal situation gone wrong, you can be prepared for anything that comes ahead by flexing your reflexes.

Being prepared for emergencies involves having the skills needed to react immediately. If there is something like a natural emergency such as a tornado, heavy thunderstorm, or snowstorm, what preparation needs to be taken for everybody's safety? In a snowstorm, you want to make sure that you let your faucets drip so that your pipes don't freeze and burst.

During a thunderstorm, keep your windows closed and avoid parking underneath any trees if you are driving a car. Stay away from the window in extremely heavy thunderstorms and have a flashlight ready to go.

In a tornado, get to the lowest level and keep your head covered, staying away from windows as you would in a thunderstorm. Visualize these situations and what you would do to get out of an emergency so that you can be prepared for anything.

BASIC FIRST AID

When we're children and we get hurt, our parents or teachers come rushing to help. As an adult, it's your responsibility to respond with the proper first aid method when sick. Keep a first aid kit in your car or in a place you can easily access at home. This can include:

- pain medicine like acetaminophen or ibuprofen
- bandages and gauze
- alcohol wipes and antiseptic cream
- tweezers
- gloves
- thermometer

Clean wounds right away to knock off any dirt or debris. Wash with water and gently let it run over the wound. Avoid scrubbing, as it might make the cut worse. Assess if you need stitches or not. Cuts deeper than half an inch might require stitches (Santos-Longhurst, 2018). If it's wide and gaping and bleeding excessively, that can also assess how bad the damage is. If stitches are needed, get to a hospital right away so that it can be properly treated to prevent infection. Wash your hands before and after touching anyone's wound.

One thing to remember is to always go to the hospital after a serious head injury, especially if consciousness is lost. While you might not feel terrible, head injuries can be serious and cause issues to arise later on.

Learning CPR is another valuable skill, especially if you ever decide to try earning cash through babysitting.

HOW TO BE A FUR-PARENT

Petting your cat or dog can actually cause a chemical reaction in your body in which oxytocin and serotonin are released. These hormones are what help provide you with happy feelings (Reeves, 2021).

Pets are great companions and can provide you with responsibility, stability, and alleviation from loneliness. Many places restrict pets, however, so never adopt before you know where you'll be living and whether or not they will let you keep your pet.

Becoming a parent of a cat or dog can teach you great responsibility. They need to follow daily schedules that involve feeding them, providing water, ensuring they can use the bathroom, and sometimes bathing or grooming them. Dogs are a little harder, as they need to be taken out multiple times a day, even when you don't feel like getting out of bed.

Though there are many ways to get a pet for free, they can bring costs after. They require vet visits, sometimes in an emergency, and this can be very expensive. They also need food, cats need litter, and both deserve things like toys and beds.

If you're a first-time fur-parent, make sure you either adopt a pet that is spayed/neutered or that you have the money to do this, along with their necessary vaccines.

They deserve to have a clean space! This means cleaning the litter box every day and potty-training dogs so they don't go in the house. Cats don't like to be dirty, and dogs will require regular bathing and grooming.

Fresh water should be available all day long, and don't forget to clean the bowl with soap and water periodically in between. While having a pet is fun, it's a huge responsibility, so never take that on if you're unsure.

BABYSITTING DO'S AND DON'TS

Babysitting is a great way to show responsibility and make some extra money as an adolescent. You can learn how to be responsible by making a commitment and showing up on time.

To start finding babysitting gigs, ask friends or inquire within social circles. You never know whose parents are looking for extra help. There are also resources for you to find jobs online, like Care.com. In some areas, 14 is the minimum age allowed, so keep that in mind.

Once you land a gig, treat it like a real job. Get there early and dress appropriately.

Keep the space clean while the parents are away, and if you can, go above and beyond and tidy up so that it's cleaner when they get home than when they left.

Know your limits and don't go too far into the house, like into the parent's bedrooms. Avoid snooping in cabinets and drawers and respect their privacy.

While babysitting, it's essential to make sure that kids are never alone at bath time. Even if the water is draining, shallow levels can be dangerous. Take classes to help you grow your babysitting skills, and take it further by dog sitting, house sitting, and even dog walking.

LEARN TO SWIM

Learning how to swim can ensure that you are not afraid of water, and this will give you confidence whenever you are hanging out with friends by a pool or lake.

Knowing how to swim could also potentially save a life, as well as serve as a fun way to stay fit (Stewart, n.d.).

Many schools offer swim lessons for those who need them. If not, look into your local community center and see if there is a pool in which you can practice.

When practicing on your own, make sure there is supervision. To master the art of swimming, follow these rules:

- Practice being able to bring yourself above the water's surface. This can be done in the shallow end so that you can stand up as needed.
- Practice controlling your movement as well as floating.
- When you are able to float, you can use your arms and legs to move through the water.
- Control your breathing and practice blowing out through your nose when submerged under water (*Become Water Competent*, n.d.).

If you're going to be around bodies of water, be careful of what you choose to wear. Heavy clothing or long skirts could weigh you down if you fall in. Always wear a life jacket on a boat, even if you're an experienced swimmer. Follow the lines created by lifeguards to avoid the dangers of a current.

If someone around you is drowning, do not go into the water to try and save them. Drowning people can be frantic and might pull you down or push you under the water. Instead, try using a long pole or throwing them a flotation device (*What To Do When Someone Is Drowning*, n.d.).

KITCHEN BASICS

The key to cooking doesn't come down to your skill level, how much you spend on ingredients, or what type of food you're cooking. Really, all it takes to make a delicious meal is having the right kitchen tools.

This starts with things you will eat and drink with on. Have at least two of the following:

- plates
- cups
- forks
- knives
- bowls

Four is preferred, and six of each is even better so that you have plenty for when guests come over.

On top of that, good cookware can help you cook things like chicken, eggs, rice, and so much more. Invest in:

- mixing bowls
- large skillet
- large pot

You can get smaller versions of these things as well, but if you only have one of each, it's good to make sure they're large so that you're not limited when cooking.

A crock pot or instant pot can make cooking at home even easier. Use wooden utensils as these are better for use with pans, and they last a long time.

Sheet pans and baking dishes are also good to have for oven use and invest in a muffin tin if you can as well.

A sharp knife and a wooden cutting board are great for chopping fresh veggies and herbs. Measuring cups, spoons, or a kitchen scale are good for baking and cooking to ensure you always use the right portions.

Finally, invest in a can and bottle opener so that you are able to actually access the food you want to cook! Once you have prepared all of these things, you can start the actual cooking process.

HOW TO COOK

Cooking at home helps you save money while also focusing on healthier options. Cooking something at home doesn't mean it's automatically healthier, but it does ensure you know exactly what is going into your meals.

A great meal is colorful and has three parts:

- grains
- proteins
- vegetables

To make it a flavorful meal, add seasonings, fresh herbs, and sauces or dips. This creates a great formula for future meals:

1 grain + 1 protein + 1 vegetable/fruit + 1 flavor enhancer = delicious meal

Fill in this formula with some basics. For example:

- brown rice + salmon + broccoli + teriyaki sauce
- sourdough bread + soft boiled egg + avocado + hot sauce
- quinoa + chicken + red pepper + hummus

Add in cheeses, more herbs, and extra veggies to make these meals even more complete.

Don't be afraid to get in the kitchen and start experimenting. So much is learned as you go and each meal helps you improve. When crafting meals and picking ingredients, it's crucial to understand nutrition labels.

READING NUTRITION LABELS

Nutrition labels are required to be on a lot of food products and can provide you with insight into where this product came from, what ingredients are inside, and which vitamins and nutrients you are receiving.

Nutrition facts contain:

- Ingredients: Be cautious of ingredients with multiple names. For example, there are over 50 names for how sugar might be listed (Barnwell, 2022)!
- Calories: Calories represent the amount it takes to burn a certain food. Most humans burn anywhere from 1,600 to 3,000 calories a day, so try to keep calories limited to how much physical activity you're getting (Fetters, 2022).
- Carbohydrates: These help to keep you energized, but some carbs have hidden sugars,

so it's important to see the breakdown of this on the label.
- Sodium: Sodium is needed in the body, but too much can be bad for you, so limit foods with high sodium levels.

There are many other things on a nutrition label, like fat, protein, and other vitamins. Reading these labels can ensure that you build balanced meals and avoid certain ingredients that might be bad for your health (FDA, 2022).

DOING THE LAUNDRY

Starting laundry as a teenager will make adult life so much easier. If you build a habit of doing your laundry, folding it, and putting it away, you will have a clean and clutter-free space.

Laundry starts by separating clothes into different categories. Separate out your socks and underwear. Towels can be a separate load as well. Both of these things can be washed with hot water to ensure they get extra clean. Hot water can make clothes fade, so it's best to wash shirts and pants with color with cold water.

Don't overstuff the machines. The water and soap need to be able to reach every piece of clothing in the machine, and stuffing it too full could mean that it can't make it to the middle. Shake out all the laundry as you put it in. Socks rolled up and pants with twisted legs might also miss getting hit with soap and water. Always check your pockets.

Hang dry shirts with decals to prevent chipping and peeling. Turn them inside out when washing so they don't fade.

Another helpful laundry tip is to stand at the machine and quickly fold the load after it's dry. This will take about 10 minutes. Taking the laundry out, putting it somewhere else, and going back to it later adds unnecessary extra steps. Before you know it, the laundry will pile up and become out of control. Maintain a clean environment and take the clothes right from the dryer, fold them, and put them away immediately. Having your clothes easily accessible will make it so much easier when it comes time to pack a suitcase.

PACKING A SUITCASE

If you plan on going away to college, you will be traveling quite frequently. It's helpful to know how to pack a suitcase so that you never forget items and can be prepared for travel with ease.

Write everything down before you go. Create your schedule so you can determine what type of clothing you need. For example, if you're going camping, you wouldn't want to pack high heels.

Try rolling your clothes to save space. It makes it easier to reach in and find things in your suitcase rather than stacked clothing, and it could prevent wrinkling.

Keep socks and underwear in a different spot in your bag, and have a backup outfit in your carry-on bag in case checked baggage gets lost in travel.

When flying, keep electronics in a different part of the bag, as these usually need to be scanned separately from the rest of your luggage. Wrap liquids in plastic, or use pajamas since these are the least essential clothes and can get a little dirtier.

It can help to create a checklist on your phone so that you can always have something to reference when packing. If one day you find you forgot something, you can add it to the list to prevent making the same mistake twice.

ORGANIZATION SKILLS

A cluttered home can increase stress, decrease focus, and negatively impact productivity (*How to Be More*

Organized, n.d.). Keeping a clean space makes it easier to find what you're looking for while freeing up your time.

One of the most effective rules to follow around the house is the two-minute rule. If a task takes less than two minutes, do it immediately! Do not put it off. If you push this off ten times throughout the day, suddenly, you have over 20 minutes of work to do. This feels like a more daunting task, making it even easier to keep pushing it off. Some tasks that take less than two minutes include:

- rinsing a dish and putting it in the dishwasher
- picking up clothes and putting them into a hamper
- making the bed (sometimes longer but still a quick task)
- tossing leftovers in the fridge
- going through mail and recycling what isn't needed

Doing these things every day will take less than ten minutes of your time. Not doing them will make the house chaotic and dirty, and that will create a big mess to tackle.

Keep paperwork and schoolwork organized in a bin. Use binders or folders to keep them separated. Keep your birth certificate, passport, and other important papers in a folder in a safe spot. Staying on top of these things and keeping yourself organized will make your life so much easier.

YARD WORK

Yard work is good for all ages; it's a chance to spend time in nature and breathe in the fresh air. When doing yard work, you can feel the sun on your skin, and it could even be a way to earn extra income if you decide to help out in your neighborhood.

Once you move away, you could even make a deal with your landlord to do some yard work in exchange for cheaper rent.

Improving your yard work skills can begin with basic plant care. Most plants need to be watered daily in the summer. Make sure to water their roots, not the leaves, and that the water spreads over them evenly.

Pull weeds to help prevent invasive plants from taking over the ornamental ones. Use mulch on top of plants to help increase aesthetics, trap moisture, and prevent pests and weeds from calling your garden their home.

As you advance, you can learn how to use things like lawnmowers and leaf blowers. Ensure you never use dangerous equipment when unsupervised.

BASIC HOUSEKEEPING SKILLS

Housekeeping isn't just for the aesthetics of your home. While an organized space can help prevent chaos from clutter, keeping your home clean goes beyond just organization. You need to clean to prevent pests, mold, and other harmful things from entering your home.

What room of your house gets the messiest on a daily basis? Chances are, it's the kitchen. We eat there all day, every day, so it's easy for the dishes to start piling up. Dishes should be done daily to prevent attracting pests. Letting them sit in the sink with food is an open invitation to fruit flies and cockroaches. Also done daily should be picking up your clothes and making your bed. If you spend just 30 minutes doing these things daily, you will notice a huge difference in how the cleanliness of your home is maintained.

Beyond these simple daily tasks, make sure to do these things at least weekly or as needed depending on how many people live in your home and how messy it gets:

- Dust surfaces like coffee tables, end tables, bookshelves, and TV stands. Pests like centipedes feed on dust and dead skin cells, not to mention dust can decrease the quality of air.
- Deep clean the bathroom. Use a cleaner that kills bacteria to wash the sink, toilet, tub, and shower. Use a toilet brush for easier cleaning of the toilet.
- Sweep and vacuum for the same reasons that you dust and do the dishes; you don't want to leave anything on the floor for hungry pests.

In addition to these tips, try to avoid waiting until the last minute to do laundry. Stay on top of it so it doesn't become another overwhelming task on your endless to-do list. Make sure everything in your home has a place so that you can always tidy up as needed. Some people enjoy cleaning, and others loathe it. Regardless of how you feel about it, some things just have to be learned, like how to unclog a toilet.

UNCLOGGING A TOILET OR SINK

The time has come. You're in the bathroom doing your normal thing. Nothing is out of the ordinary, but you've never used this toilet. You go to flush after a long day of holding it in, and suddenly the water, and everything in it, starts to rise. The toilet looks like it's going to overflow! What do you do?

The best thing to do in this situation is to use a plunger to unclog the toilet before it overflows. Take the plunger and place the rubber part over the hole in the toilet. Press down hard and lift up and down quickly without lifting the plunger off the bottom of the toilet. This helps create suction to adjust everything you flushed so that it can go down smoothly. If you don't have a plunger, you can try using a wire hanger to help break up the clog. The same trick can be used if your sink is clogged.

While it might not work for a toilet, you can also try pouring down vinegar and baking soda to help break up clogs. If you try multiple methods and nothing is working, it's best to reach out to a professional to ensure you don't cause further damage.

KNOWING WHAT SNAIL MAIL IS!

One of the most life-changing inventions on the internet has been the ability to send and receive mail instantaneously. You can email friends, companies, and coworkers— you can even email yourself! Despite all the benefits granted with this, it's important to remember what snail mail is. This is the United States Postal Service.

As a taxpayer, you will need this to communicate with the IRS, the internal revenue service. Having physical mail can establish your address and place of residence. You can also use it to show loved ones you care. Who doesn't love to get a card in the mail on their birthday?

All mail requires a stamp, and the heavier the package, the more stamps it will require. When filling out an envelope, write the full address of the destination in the middle of the envelope. Make it clear and easy to read. Your return address goes in the top left, the stamp on the top right.

Drop it in the mailbox or at the post office. If you drop it in a public mailbox, like the blue kind on the street, double-check that it fell in, as sometimes it can get stuck in the lid. You never know when you might need to mail something, so it's good to familiarize yourself with the mailing system.

WHEN GPS FAILS, KNOW HOW TO READ A MAP

Map reading isn't something that you will have to do often unless you decide to pursue a hobby surrounding nature or traveling. However, it's always good to know how to read a map just in case GPS fails you. Sometimes you might be in an area you're unfamiliar with, or maybe your phone died as you're driving home late one night. Maps are also useful for using public transportation, as sometimes you have to make decisions quicker than your phone's map can load.

Once you find a map, make sure the orientation is right. Use the sun if you are unsure of what direction you are facing. The sun rises in the east and sets in the west.

Use cross streets first and pay attention to the direction of the road so that you know which is the correct way to head.

Check the scale when you are hiking and deciding which trails to follow. Some paths look small and easy, but that's because you see a handheld version of reality. Pay attention to these small details to ensure that you don't end up embarking on a five-mile journey when you only have time for a short walk. All in all, this skill is a great metaphor for everything in life; always have a plan B, and focus on going in the right direction in life.

LEARNING TO DRIVE

Eight teenagers die a day from motor vehicle crashes (CDC, 2022). Many more are injured and traumatized in these accidents. Males have a higher risk of dying, and having a passenger also increases the risk of an accident.

According to the Center for Disease Control, the main reasons for accidents include:

- inexperience
- weekend driving
- lack of seatbelts
- distracted driving
- speeding

It goes without saying that learning how to drive safely could be the difference between life and death. Drive slowly, especially if you are inexperienced. Avoid high-traffic areas as you continue to learn and grow your confidence behind the wheel.

Reduce distractions. If you are driving multiple people in the car, make sure everyone has a seatbelt. Keep the music turned down, and set boundaries so that others are respectful and don't distract you.

In addition to learning how to drive safely, familiarize yourself with a few basics about car maintenance:

- Check wiper fluid and change your wipers when winter comes and it starts to snow.
- Have someone teach you how to change a tire, or at least watch a video so that you can familiarize yourself if ever needed.
- Learn how to check your oil and get it changed promptly once the light comes on to do so.

If you ever find that you do get into an accident, pull over and remain calm. Take pictures and call the police to file a report. If the other person is aggressive, remain in your car as long as the damage is minimal, and you can ensure that it's safe to do so.

Driving is a privilege, not a right. If you are irresponsible, you can lose that privilege, so make smart decisions when getting behind the wheel.

YOUNG MECHANIC

It's good to be handy. Once you move away from your parents, you might have to deal with household issues on your own. Knowing how to use basic tools will give you the skills to fix minor repairs and take charge of your household.

Hammers are important for hanging things and driving nails into wood for various projects. You can hang nails around your home for decorations or hanging canopies. If you want to hang something heavier, like a hanging plant or mounting a TV, you will need drywall screws. These sometimes require a drill. Drills make screwing things in easier, but they're a little more expensive.

A cheaper alternative is an actual screwdriver, which comes in different sizes. Investing in a basic tool kit can help you prepare when issues arise. Keep a stepladder around the house. You never know if you will need to change a light bulb or reach something in a high cabinet.

CHAPTER 6 REFLECTION

Answer these questions one last time, not just for this chapter, but for them all. After making it through all of the chapters, ask yourself:

- What lesson stood out the most?
- What is the importance of learning these skills?

Journal/Activities

For the first reflection activity, go back to the beginning of your journal and review your goals. Has anything changed? Even just a day is enough time to notice a difference in the way you might be thinking.

Next, reflect on how you're operating in the space around you now. Is it organized or chaotic? Does it feel like home, and if not, how can you make it better?

Finally, look back on your childhood. What is something that you have already learned about life? What is something you wish you had known five years ago? Learning to reflect in this way will help keep you focused on what matters.

Summary

When everything in life is stressful, there's nothing better than coming home to a place that makes you feel safe and happy. Though you might not have your own house, apartment, or even bedroom, it's important to find a space you can make feel like your own. Maintain a clean space and continue to familiarize yourself with basic handiness skills so that you can feel confident taking responsibility for your own space.

As we reflect on the final chapter, it's important not to feel too overwhelmed with everything you learned. You might've been able to finish the book and journals in a few days, but living through these experiences will stretch over weeks, months, and years. Learning these things has simply given you an extra boost to make the journey through the future a little easier to navigate.

Notes

SPREAD THE CONFIDENCE!

Everyone deserves to feel confident about the future… and you can help other young people like you to step into adulthood with that feeling.

Simply by sharing your honest opinion of this book on Amazon, you'll show other readers where they can find all the information they need to feel confident about growing up.

Thank you so much for your support. I'm so excited about the future you're about to create for yourself.

Scan the QR code for a quick review!

CONCLUSION

There will come a point in your future when you look back on all that you've experienced, and a realization will hit you. This epiphany will come randomly and without warning, but it will make you feel whole. You will look back on everything that you've survived with the confidence to say, "I did that."

When you are cleaning up your first home, helping your future children take their first steps, or simply laughing around a dinner table with your friends, you will look around and thank yourself for all that you've done to help you get to that exact place.

The fear of the unknown is scary for most people. While that fear looks different for everyone, the results of that anxiety can be similar. Nothing should stop you from achieving your dreams and living your life to the fullest, no matter how afraid of the future you are.

Even taking the initiative to come to this book and take hold of your future shows that you are capable of making great changes in your life. Unfortunately, many adults aren't even able to have the guts to look at their life, want to do better, and strive to get more.

There will be some rough patches in your future, no matter how much you prepare. Becoming an adult means facing heartbreak, mental health struggles, and sometimes even loss or tragedy. Major setbacks and unexpected obstacles are likely to drop into your life. These surprises will come at times you're happy and times when your plate is already filled with other stressors.

This isn't anything to fear; it's a reality we have to prepare for. No one wants to go through struggles in life, but being ready for anything will make it easier to work through the damage that some setbacks might cause.

You are not alone in this life; many of the people around you are going through the same thing, but not everyone is ready to open up and face these issues. Putting emotions into words and words into actions can be a complex process, so it's normal if you find yourself riding more of an emotional roller coaster rather than a smooth and straight road. Just know that no matter how bumpy the ride, you have created a vessel of knowledge that will always push you through.

Now that you know the whys, whats, and hows of critical life skills to thrive in the real world, it's time you apply them. Start the discussion by leaving a review! Share what stuck out to you the most, or leave some ideas for what else you want to learn about that wasn't covered in the book. What are you afraid of, and what will you do to alleviate that fear?

Opening up and sharing these things with other people will help you not only gain control over your struggles, but it will help you find people who relate to you so that you can create a strong system of support. Navigating this world is hard enough on your own, so never be afraid to reach out to others when you feel like no one understands you.

Most importantly, always remember that you can do whatever you put your mind to. The voice in your head telling you that you aren't good enough is wrong. You have the power and confidence to create the brightest future that you see ahead. There's no better time to start walking toward that future than now.

REFERENCES

APA. (2020). *Resilience for teens: 10 tips to build skills on bouncing back from rough times.* American Psychological Association. https://www.apa.org/topics/resilience/bounce-teens

Alan Cohen. (n.d.). AZQuotes. https://www.azquotes.com/quote/525648

Andrade, S. (2021). *The importance of setting healthy boundaries.* Forbes. https://www.forbes.com/sites/forbescoachescouncil/2021/07/01/the-importance-of-setting-healthy-boundaries/?sh=4b9b511b56e4

Ayuob, M. (2021). *5 ways slimming screen time is good for your health.* Mayo Clinic Health System. https://www.mayoclinichealthsystem.org/hometown-health/featured-topic/5-ways-slimming-screen-time-is-good-for-your-health

Barnwell, A. (2022). *Secret sugars: 56 different names for sugar.* Virta. https://www.virtahealth.com/blog/names-for-sugar#:

Become water competent. (n.d.). Water Safety USA. https://www.watersafetyusa.org/water-competency.html#:

Begody, C. (2023). *Teen spending habits statistics for 2023.* Lexington Law. https://www.lexingtonlaw.com/blog/credit-cards/teen-spending-habits.html

Berman, J. (2013). *Nearly half of American households are 1 emergency away from financial disaster, report finds.* Huffington Post. https://www.huffpost.com/entry/financial-emergency-report_n_2576326

Boys & girls Clubs of America. (2022). *The importance of goal-setting for teens.* Boys & Girls Clubs of America. https://www.bgca.org/news-stories/2022/January/the-importance-of-goal-setting-for-teens

CDC. (2021). *About mental health.* Centers for Disease Control and Prevention. https://www.cdc.gov/mentalhealth/learn/index.htm

Campbell, C. (2011). *Never spend your money before you have it.* Monticello. https://www.monticello.org/research-education/blog/never-spend-your-money-before-you-have-it/

Cherry, K. (2022). *Emotions and types of emotional responses.* Verywell Mind. https://www.verywellmind.com/what-are-emotions-2795178

Cherry, K. (2023). *What is self-awareness?* Verywell Mind. https://www.verywellmind.com/what-is-self-awareness-2795023

Christian, L. (2020). *Taking action: 15 smart ways to go from dreaming to doing.* Soul Salt. https://soulsalt.com/taking-action/

Confucius C. & Legge J. (1971). *Confucian analects; the great learning and the doctrine of the mean.* Dover Publications

Darn, S. (2007). *The role of homework.* British Council. https://www.teachingenglish.org.uk/professional-development/teachers/managing-resources/articles/role-homework

Dowshen, S. (2018). *Health insurance basics.* TeensHealth. https://kidshealth.org/en/teens/insurance.html

Dunham, S., Lee, E., & Persky, A. M. (2020). The Psychology of Following Instructions and Its Implications. *American journal of pharmaceutical education, 84*(8), ajpe7779. https://doi.org/10.5688/ajpe7779

Earl Nightingale. (n.d.). Goodreads. https://www.goodreads.com/quotes/362597-we-are-all-self-made-but-only-the-successful-will-admit

11 facts about high school dropout rates. (n.d.). Do Something. https://www.dosomething.org/us/facts/11-facts-about-high-school-dropout-rates

Ellis, K. (2022). *How do student loans work?.* Ramsey. https://www.ramseysolutions.com/debt/how-do-student-loans-work

Emotional Health. (n.d.). Nemours Teens Health. https://kidshealth.org/en/teens/eq.html

Expressing your feelings. (n.d.). Kids Helpline. https://kidshelpline.com.au/teens/issues/expressing-your-feelings

FDA. (n.d.). *How to understand and use the nutrition facts label.* Food and Drug Administration. https://www.fda.gov/food/new-nutrition-facts-label/how-understand-and-use-nutrition-facts-label

Fetters, A. (2022). *A scientifically proven way to lose 1 pound of weight.*

Everyday Health. https://www.everydayhealth.com/weight/how-to-achieve-one-pound-of-weight-loss.aspx#:

Finding the right tone of voice in communication. (2020). Harappa. https://harappa.education/harappa-diaries/tone-of-voice-types-and-examples-in-communication/

Harvard Health. (n.d.). *Benefits of mindfulness.* Help Guide. https://www.helpguide.org/harvard/benefits-of-mindfulness.htm

Heldt, A. (2021). *The importance of community service in a teen's life.* The Bridge Teen Center. https://thebridgeteencenter.org/news/the-importance-of-community-service-in-a-teens-life

Hitchens C. (2001). *Letters to a young contrarian.* Basic Books.

How to avoid debt. (n.d.). American Consumer Credit Counseling. https://www.consumercredit.com/debt-resources-tools/videos/informational-videos/how-to-avoid-debt/

How to be more organized. (n.d.). Mind Tools. https://www.mindtools.com/auj8unv/how-to-be-more-organized

Johns Hopkins Medicine. (n.d.). *Healthy eating during adolescence.* John Hopkins Medicine. https://www.hopkinsmedicine.org/health/wellness-and-prevention/healthy-eating-during-adolescence

Johnson, D. (2019). *The importance of taking the perspective of others.* Psychology Today. https://www.psychologytoday.com/us/blog/constructive-controversy/201906/the-importance-taking-the-perspective-others

Kindness matters guide. (n.d.). Mental Health Foundation. https://www.mentalhealth.org.uk/explore-mental-health/kindness/kindness-matters-guide

Lake, M. (2018). *The importance of social skills: raising a socially intelligent child.* Good Therapy. https://www.goodtherapy.org/blog/importance-of-social-skills-raising-socially-intelligent-child-0102184

Lake, R. (2022). *Guide to allowances and kids.* Investopedia. https://www.investopedia.com/guide-allowances-and-kids-5217591

Linwood, A. (n.d.). *Allowance and money management.* Encyclopedia. https://www.encyclopedia.com/medicine/encyclopedias-almanacs-transcripts-and-maps/allowance-and-money-management

Mayo Clinic. (2022). *Forgiveness: letting go of grudges and bitterness.* Mayo Clinic. https://www.mayoclinic.org/healthy-lifestyle/adult-health/in-depth/forgiveness/art-20047692

Morin, A. (2021). *Steps to good decision making skills for teens.* Verwell Family. https://www.verywellfamily.com/steps-to-good-decision-making-skills-for-teens-2609104#citation-4

Morin, A. (2023). *10 things to do when you feel alone.* Verywell Mind. https://www.verywellmind.com/things-to-do-if-you-feel-lonely-5081371

Newman, K. (2016). *Four reasons to cultivate patience.* Greater Good Magazine. https://greatergood.berkeley.edu/article/item/four_reasons_to_cultivate_patience

Ohio University. (2022). *What is the value of teamwork?.* Ohio University. https://onlinemasters.ohio.edu/blog/what-is-the-value-of-teamwork/

Opperman, M. (n.d.). *What's a good credit score?* Credit Score Ranges Explained. Credit.org. https://credit.org/blog/what-is-a-good-credit-score-infographic/

O'Shea, B. and Schwahn, L. (2022). *Budgeting 101: how to budget money.* Nerd Wallet. https://www.nerdwallet.com/article/finance/how-to-budget

PennState Extension. (n.d.). *Leadership and children.* PennState Extension. https://extension.psu.edu/programs/betterkidcare/early-care/tip-pages/all/leadership-and-children

Peter Shepherd. (n.d.). AZQuotes.com. https://www.azquotes.com/quote/1033078

Pickhardt, C. (2014). *Adolescence and commitment.* Psychology Today. https://www.psychologytoday.com/us/blog/surviving-your-childs-adolescence/201403/adolescence-and-commitment

Reeves, K. (2020). *The importance of pets in our lives.* Transitions Life Care. https://www.transitionslifecare.org/2020/05/27/the-importance-of-pets-in-our-lives/

Rejection and how to handle it. (n.d.). TeensHealth. https://kidshealth.org/en/teens/rejection.html

Rittenberg, M. (n.d.). *The importance of authenticity.* Berkeley Exec Ed.

https://executive.berkeley.edu/thought-leadership/blog/importance-authenticity

Rockwood, K. (2020). *Banking 101: understanding how banks work*. Step. https://step.com/money-101/post/a-teens-guide-to-banking

Roth, E. (2019). *Self-defense for teens: tips, techniques and advice*. Metro Parent. https://www.metroparent.com/parenting/tweens-teens/self-defense-for-teens-tips-techniques-and-advice/

Santos-Longhurst, A. (2018). *Do I need stitches? How to tell if you need medical care*. Healthline. https://www.healthline.com/health/when-to-get-stitches

Schilling, D. (2012). *10 steps to effective listening*. Forbes. https://www.forbes.com/sites/womensmedia/2012/11/09/10-steps-to-effective-listening/?sh=5b1499c33891

Self-esteem. (2022). Mind. https://www.mind.org.uk/information-support/types-of-mental-health-problems/self-esteem/tips-to-improve-your-self-esteem/

Selig, M. (2018). *6 ways to discover and choose your core values*. Psychology Today. https://www.psychologytoday.com/us/blog/changepower/201811/6-ways-discover-and-choose-your-core-values

Sigsworth, L. (2020). *Creative thinking: video tips for developing teenagers' creativity*. Cambridge. https://www.cambridge.org/elt/blog/2020/07/07/creative-thinking-video-tips-for-developing-teenagers-creativity/

Sigsworth, L. (2020, June 24). *Critical thinking video tips to develop teens*. Cambridge English Blog. https://www.cambridge.org/elt/blog/2020/06/24/critical-thinking-video-tips-to-develop-teens/

Sonnenberg, F. (2016). *The importance of good manners*. Drake University. https://raycenter.wp.drake.edu/2018/04/17/the-importance-of-good-manners/

Stewart, T. (n.d.). *Why is it important to know how to swim?*. Live Strong. https://www.livestrong.com/article/457393-why-is-it-important-to-know-how-to-swim/

Suni, E. (2023). *Teens and sleep*. Sleep Foundation. https://www.sleepfoundation.org/teens-and-sleep

The basics: essential kitchen tools. (n.d.). Cook Smarts. https://www.cooks

marts.com/cooking-guides/create-a-functional-kitchen/20-must-have-kitchen-tools/

Twain, M. (1982). *Mark Twain.* New York, Greenwich House

University of Rochester. (n.d.). *Exercise and teenagers.* University of Rochester. https://www.urmc.rochester.edu/encyclopedia/content.aspx?ContentTypeID=90&ContentID=P01602

University of South Carolina. (n.d.). *Dating safely.* University of South Carolina. https://sc.edu/about/offices_and_divisions/law_enforcement_and_safety/safety-on-campus/dating-safety/index.php

Webster, I. (2023). *$1 in 1920 is worth $13.33 today.* Official Data. https://www.officialdata.org/ca/inflation/1920?amount=1

Welker, E. (2010). *Decision making/problem solving with teens.* Ohioline. https://ohioline.osu.edu/factsheet/HYG-5301

What to do when someone is drowning. (n.d.). Health Exchange. https://www.healthxchange.sg/heart-lungs/lung-conditions/what-to-do-when-someone-is-drowning#:

Why hobbies are important? (2019). Kettering Global. https://online.kettering.edu/news/2019/04/15/why-hobbies-are-important

Winter, M. (2021). *Nine in 10 parents say teens lack domestic skills - from ironing to vacuuming.* Mirror. https://www.mirror.co.uk/lifestyle/family/teens-lack-domestic-life-skills-25096590

Young, Colten. (2020). *Focus: the science of self-control.* Life Intelligence. https://www.lifeintelligence.io/blog/focus-the-science-of-self-control

Feyoh, M. (2023, March 16). 45 quotes about growing up to inspire you or your children. Develop Good Habits. https://www.developgoodhabits.com/quotes-about-growing-up/

Made in the USA
Columbia, SC
28 March 2024